Contents

Contents

Longman
London and New York

Longman Group Limited,
Longman House,
Burnt Mill, Harlow,
Essex CM20 2JE,
England
and Associated Companies
throughout the World.

Published in the United States of America
by Longman Inc., New York.

First published in 1984
© Longman Group Ltd. 1984

British Library Cataloguing in Publication Data

Kayongo-Male, Diane
 The sociology of the African family.
 1. Family – Social aspects – Africa
 I. Title   II. Onyango, Philista
 306.8'5'096   HQ728
 ISBN 0–582–64703–7

Library of Congress Cataloging in Publication Data

Kayongo-Male, Diane.
 The sociology of the African family.
 Bibliography: p.
 Includes index.
 1. Family – Africa. 2. Family policy – Africa.
 I. Onyango, Philista. II. Title
 HQ691.K39 1984   306.8'5'096   84-807
 ISBN 0-582-64703-7

Set in Times (Linotron)

Printed in Hong Kong
by Wing Lee Printing Co Ltd

1 Introduction: the family in Africa

This textbook on the sociology of the African family is intended to fill a gap in teaching materials on the continent. Although families all over the world do have similarities, African students, lecturers and scholars often find Western textbooks on the family unsuitable for a full understanding of the dynamics of African family life. What is vitally needed are more books and research on African family life from a sociological point of view.

Anthropological work on African family life is abundant. This book, however, makes no attempt to review all the vast literature. First of all, it would be impossible to do justice to all of it in a book of this length, and secondly, our emphasis is on sociological concepts and processes rather than on anthropological ones. Although we do not advocate rigid disciplinarianism, the fact is that sociological books on the African family are scarce and there are no current sociological works dealing comprehensively with family life for the whole of black Africa. This book deals with black African families, south of the Sahara, ignoring the Indian and European racial groupings, and attempts to suggest common features and processes of African families.

Although the title of the book mentions the African family, we do not try to describe a so-called 'ideal-type' family. There are many variations in African family life. Yet more detailed country studies need to be done in order fully to record or describe current variations. Only when such studies are complete could anyone be bold enough to attempt a general synthesis, an ideal type or a theory of the African family. Our aim is merely to summarize what is known about African family life in terms of a general sociology of the family framework.

We begin with a general overview of the social setting of Africa, and review some basic features of the African family. After a detailed examination of the family in Africa, in both its internal functioning and in its interrelationships with external agencies, the book closes with some 'theoretical considerations'. Evolving from the substance of African family life, the chapter on theoretical considerations suggests possible emphases for general sociological theorizing on the African family.

The setting

European and Arab contact with Africa initiated highly disruptive changes which affected African family life. New economic systems changed family production systems; political actions led to forced labour, racial segregation and alienation of land – all of which had implications for family life; and religious proselytization altered the symbolic meaning of family life. Because both the earlier slave-trade period and the colonial period were justified by racist ideas which assumed that Africans had no family life, no culture and no civilization, slavery and all other experiences could not be destroying what did not exist! These racist notions persisted even when academic scholarship began on the continent. 'Native' studies often contained elaborate details of exotic rituals and the 'sexual life of savages' instead of details of the symbolic and social meaning of family life.

The colonialists also created or increased conflict among ethnic groups which has lasted until our time. The majority of current refugees are a result of this type of conflict. Family life for refugees is understandably difficult and tragic for many, being isolated from their traditions and dependent upon the donations of others. Inequalities created during the colonial period tend to breed a series of military governments, some of which (as in Amin's Uganda) led to killing and destruction. Uganda's recently created special programme for widows is intended to cater for family problems resulting from years of social and political instability.

Health problems were magnified over time as new diseases were introduced into the continent. Family health deteriorated, particularly in areas where large tracts of land were alienated. Forced labour interfered with family farming when members of the household were periodically withdrawn from the farms. Creations like the Bantustans of South Africa and the urban 'bed-space' housing of colonial Kenya made it impossible for families to live together. Often the health status of families left behind in the reserves or village areas deteriorated due to malnutrition.

Schools founded by the colonialists led to rifts within families as the educated members began to question the authority of the uneducated, older members of the family. Authority patterns were also disrupted, with women experiencing the greatest losses, when land titles were individualized and men took over the title deeds. Recently, researchers like Van Allen (1972) have shown that African women often had a great deal of power over men in the pre-colonial period. She explains that in the 'sitting on a man' activity, women gathered together to sing songs about men who behaved badly. They were thus able to alter unacceptable male behaviour through public abuse.

Some of the traditional ceremonies were hidden during the more oppressive phases of colonialism, and returned to public life with independence. There were parts of Africa that remained relatively untouched, but most parts were affected in various ways.

Revolutionary struggles and independence movements finally freed most of Africa, but not before rapid, almost uncontrollable changes had been set in motion. Revolutionary governments enacted more sweeping changes to counter the effects of colonialism, such as equalizing the role of women in society, reducing the woman's burden of work in the family and equitably distributing resources so that all families would have fair life chances. However, all independent governments were faced with numerous, almost insurmountable problems and family problems were usually the last to be addressed in national development plans. There is as yet no African country with an explicit, comprehensive family policy.

Currently, family life in Africa is beset by special problems. Many families live in dire poverty in urban squatter areas, subsisting through work in the informal sector. Children of the poor become wage labourers, even though legislation usually prohibits it, or they become beggars on the streets of the major towns. Famine camps contain another large proportion of families, for which psychological counselling as well as stable food supplies are needed before these families can even think of a normal family life.

The World Health Organization has recently started a special research programme on tropical diseases – Africa harbours all these diseases in abundance. Some of these, like malaria and bilharzia, frustrate efforts to improve the life of the poor by draining the strength of millions. Infant and child mortality rates are high due to malnutrition and lowered resistance because of the contraction of major diseases. Education for family life includes educating mothers on how to grow more nutritional foods and basic health knowledge.

Pastoral groups are very distinctive in their way of family life, and they have recently been confronted by problems like famine, a very high level of cattle losses, and attempts at sedentarization. They are often the most traditional groups in the society. Sedentarization involves changes in the division of labour, in authority patterns and in socialization patterns, to mention only the most obvious. We do not attempt to deal specifically with pastoral family life for the following reasons: these groups are very much in the minority on the continent; the length of this book does not allow proper coverage of relevant details; and their way of life has been so drastically threatened in recent years that what we write is likely to be outdated in a very short time.

Finally, class distinctions have begun to differentiate family life. There is, however, no comparable data for all classes on most sub-topics in this book, but some effort is made to summarize how class affects family life.

Characteristics of African family life

African families can be thought of in terms of both the classical or more traditional forms as well as the more modern forms. There is also reference in this textbook to Western or conjugal types of families. For our purposes, 'Western' and 'conjugal' are considered as largely equivalent terms, though we do realize that the term 'Western' is particularly problematic. There are indeed many varieties of Western families, yet in current usage the term has come to refer to the conjugal type of family. Rather than enter into a possibly confusing debate, we prefer simply to indicate that whereas the conjugal type is the most theoretically specific term, having been elaborated upon by William Goode, it would not enable us to fully deal with the range of characteristics associated with the modern African family – hence, the use of the term 'modern' to refer to the modern African family as described below.

We begin with examples of the more traditional African family and proceed to the modern African family. Anthropologists have provided numerous descriptions of traditional African family life. We have selected from these descriptions in order to highlight particular features of the family and also to illustrate how diverse the traditional systems were. African families have often had bridewealth, polygyny and patrilocal residence as significant features. Our first example is the Swazi people of Swaziland, where polygyny was the ideal. Young men set up their houses in the same general area as their brothers. The transfer of the *lobola*, the bridewealth, in cattle, in various stages, formalized the marriage. The *lobola* gave the husband's group the right to all children borne by the woman. Each wife had her own hut, farmlands and cattle. Although the pattern of residence was patrilocal, no familiarity was allowed between the sons' wives and the father-in-law. Strict avoidance between the wives and the father-in-law parallels the custom in many African family systems (Kuper, 1965).

Secondly, the pastoral Fulani family illustrates the gradualness of the African marriage process, or rather the number of ceremonies over time instead of any one specific ceremony marking the beginning of a marriage. Girls were often betrothed before their first menstruation. This was done through a verbal promise between parents. There were then two or three public sacrifices of cows, with the girl herself being uninvolved. The girl and boy referred to each other as husband and wife once the cows were sacrificed. Until she menstruated, the girl continued to meet young people and to perform her daily tasks. At first menstruation she was secluded and then began avoidance of all social interaction with males (Dupire, 1963).

Sometime after her seclusion, the girl was 'captured' by one of her groom's brothers, and taken reluctantly as her family waged a mock struggle to keep her. When she arrived at her parents-in-law's compound, she was given a mat to sleep on, which was her only home until she gave birth. In the last stage of pregnancy she returned home to her own parents to give birth and remained until the child was about two years old. Then, when the husband sent for her she returned to his village and was provided with a proper house and was for the first time treated as a woman and accepted as a true wife (Dupire, 1963).

There are groups which had a type of matrilocal residence for the early married years, followed by patrilocal residence. For instance, among the !Kung people the woman's separation from her parents came a long time after she was married. This happened because of the custom of bride service, whereby the husband worked for the wife's parents for a specified period. Apparently, there was no bridewealth; the work involved usually being hunting. After the required period, the wife and husband went to live permanently with the husband's people. The wife's parents were not disadvantaged after the departure of their sons or son-in-law since their own sons similarly returned home with their wives and children after completing their bride service (Marshall, 1965).

A practice which was common among the rural Hausa provides a contrast to the bride service of the !Kung. *Gandu*, a farming relationship between father and son, meant that a son would live with his parents for a long period, sometimes until the father's death. By working for the father, alongside the family's slaves, the son earned many benefits and was able to build up his own wealth. However, any son-in-*gandu* could not have more than one wife. When the father died, the farms were passed on to the sons who may have by then had sons of their own who could work for them in a *gandu* relationship. Most wives did not do farm work because of Islamic seclusion rules, so that this *gandu* relationship was of central importance to the success of the household (Hill, 1972).

Finally, matrilineal descent was practised among some groups, although it is declining in many parts of the continent. One example of matrilineal descent is the Plateau Tonga group. In the Tonga family, a man had little authority over his wife since she was largely under the authority of her mother's brother. The man's sons could not inherit from him. Instead, the mother's clan handled all its members' property and allocated or distributed property after a member's death. In a contrasting example, among the matrilineal Akan of Ghana, the men have the right to make wills which enable them to pass on their property to their sons (Mair, 1974). Finally, a third matrilineal group is the Abouré of the Ivory Coast. This group demands only a small bridewealth payment by the groom's family, but also a dowry from the bride's family. The wife's loyalties are primarily with her brothers. Her children inherit from her eldest brother. Patrilocal residence is the custom, and the wife is expected to provide some limited help to her mother-in-law. Divorce occurs very often, as in many other matrilineal systems where the woman has more rights or benefits from her own family than from her husband.

Few of the classical or traditional African family forms have remained unchanged. However, it is difficult to know, given the sparsity of data on family change, which forms or life styles have changed in recent years and exactly how they have changed.

We now turn to the characteristics of the modern African family. Harrell-Bond's (1976) study in Sierra Leone of family stereotypes is one of the more comprehensive summaries of African family life. Being stereotypes we must be cautious in interpreting the results, since stereotypes are by their very nature not accurate measures of reality, and in fact are often distortions of reality. Even with the acknowledged problem in using stereotypes we can learn a lot about people's views about differences between African and Western family life.

The stereotypes of African family life include the following features: no public display of affection between spouses; strong parental authority; family care for the elderly; cooperation between relatives; no assistance from the husband in domestic work; involvement of parents in the choice of spouse; polygamy; no marriage ceremony; early marriage for women; large families living together; no courtship; little privacy; no emphasis on love-making; payment of bridewealth; no freedom of communication between parents and children; families not eating together as a group; children reared by a large number of relatives; marriage based on economic motives; and families not sharing leisure. For the Western family, the stereotypes are all the opposites of the above, with the exception of polygamy, where monogamy is the Western attribute; and the Western marriage is based on love. We cannot be sure of the frequency with which the traits mentioned for African families are indeed found in the African family. However, most of these traits are typical features of African family life, the more traditional families possessing more of the features than the more modern families.

We now examine some of the common characteristics in more detail. The most significant feature of African family life is probably the *importance of the larger kin group* beyond the nuclear family. Inheritance was commonly the communal variety wherein the entire kin group owns the land. In many parts of the continent bridewealth is still paid to the family of the bride, with the resulting marriage linking two families rather than simply the bride and the groom. Conflicts between husband and wife were mediated by relatives instead of being sorted out privately by the couple.

Members of the extended family still have a lot of say about the marriages of their younger relatives. These family members are also linked in strong reciprocal aid relationships which entail complex rights and responsibilities. Households in urban areas have extended kin members in residence for years. The relatives may or may not be contributing financially or in terms of helping in the division of family labour, yet they are allowed to remain. Children may go to live with distant relatives for schooling or special training courses. Relatives may also have much influence over the decisions of the couple.

A second feature is the *importance of children* to the total kin group. Children were so important that husbands were allowed to marry a number of wives to guard against being childless. Even today a childless marriage is thought of as a troublesome one since marriage seems meaningless without children.

Understandably, artificial means of family planning have been a type of 'diffusionless' innovation in some respects. The health of the child had traditionally been protected by long periods of abstinence from sexual relationships when the child was breast feeding. Among the East African ethnic groups, it was believed that sexual intercourse spoiled the milk and hence harmed the child (Kabwegyere, 1977:206). In Yoruba society, the duration of post-partum sexual abstinence was normally three years. It was common for the wife to return to her family of origin during this period (Orubuloye, 1981a:57). Thus, families were spaced through such practices as abstinence and physical separation of husband and wife. It was shown in Togo recently that 66 per cent of the women interviewed were still willing to observe a 1 to 3 year period of abstinence (Kumekpor, 1970:15). Most women do not use any artificial means to limit the number of children. In Ibadan, for example, only 7 per cent of the married women had intentionally and successfully restricted fertility to six births or less (Caldwell, 1977:95).

Large numbers of children are highly valued, and family planning is antithetical to the common notion that children are a gift from God. Traditional abstinence was intended to ensure the health of children but not to reduce the number of children. Even the urban elites in places like

Ife, Oyo and Lagos have a mean ideal family size of from 4 to 6 children. Furthermore, 'Olusanya has indicated that fertility increases' with urban residence and with education among the Yoruba (Adepoju, 1977:137–38).

Both levirate and woman–woman marriage were other means of insuring that children were born and the family line continued. Levirate is the practice whereby a brother inherits the widow of his deceased brother. Levirate was partly intended as a way of protecting the woman and her children, but also served to beget children in cases where a man died leaving no children. These children were referred to as if they had been fathered by the deceased. Although some writers argue that levirate is unique to Africa, this is mistaken since it was practised by the Jews as described in the Bible in Deuteronomy.

Woman-to-woman marriage is found in some parts of East and Central Africa. Krige (1974:11) defines this as the 'institution by which a woman gives bridewealth for and marries a woman, over whom and whose offspring she has full control, delegating to a male genitor the duties of procreation'. The woman who gives the bridewealth may be either married or unmarried depending on the ethnic group. The genitor is in some systems chosen by the woman–husband, and in other cultural systems is chosen by the woman–wife.

The practice is found among such groups as the Nuer, the Akamba and the Lovedu, and in Dahomey. Such marriages served a number of purposes. In Dahomey, a barren wife could save her position in the family by using her property to obtain a wife for her husband, with the children of this union becoming her children. It was also connected with the need to build up an individual house and the need to obtain sufficient labour. There were no sexual connotations for the two women. The relationship was designed largely to raise children in the name of the 'woman–husband' and to establish a secure economic or political position through these children. It has been shown that the role of female husband, in some groups, served to enable the woman to take on male political positions or powerful occupations such as diviners or curers (O'Brien, 1977). There were women who were married but had to leave their marriages and also become female husbands before they could accept certain political offices.

Bringing up children served to perpetuate the family name and maintain the link between the ancestors and the living. The children would eventually be in charge of remembering the dead through maintenance of family shrines or in other ways. Children belonged to the parents but also to the kin group, but this did not mean the type of possessiveness over children manifested by parents in Western societies. Children were and often are sent to live with relatives for years without parents worrying about how the children are being raised. Children were used to show kinship solidarity, and giving them up to others often meant that parents were willing to share their precious gift with other relatives, especially childless ones. Children were a sign of God's blessing though they also had pratical value in terms of their potential labour contributions.

Lack of public display of affection is a third feature. This is one of the more resilient features of African family life. Whether in front of friends, relatives or children, husband and wife are not supposed to express their affection for each other. In a way, affection is expressed through respect and caring for each other's needs in subtle ways. However, holding hands or kissing in public are frowned upon. It was the belief in some groups that the wife who was well taken care of by her husband was a physically ample one, whereas a mistreated wife was thin and tired-looking. Such subtle attitudes may indicate a deeper feeling than various types of more direct, open or verbal behaviour that is intended to demonstrate feeling.

Care for and respect for the elderly, especially one's parents, are still very important in African families. Whatever the position of the child, he is expected to treat the elderly with great respect. Assistance must be given to make their less productive years trouble-free.

There is also the characteristic in African families of *little privacy* between spouses, especially if relatives are resident with the couple. In a sense, this means that the couple has little time to spend alone together.

Both the *de-emphasis on love or love-making* as well as the *constrained communication between parents and children* are on the decline as more people become educated. Many people choose their own spouses and inform their parents of their intention to marry. Educated parents tend to have freer communication with their children than those who are uneducated.

Lack of a marriage ceremony is one of the more misleading stereotypes in the African family. Although it is true that one ceremony is often not enough to create an African marriage, it is not accurate to say there is no ceremony. As noted earlier, there are many ceremonies, extending the marriage process over time, rather than the Western practice of having only one ceremony taking a matter of an hour or less to formalize the marriage of two individuals. Thus, in terms of traditional African marriages, the formalization of the marriage was based on a series of interrelated ceremonies or steps rather than a single ceremony. Much of the emphasis on a large single ceremony has emerged in the last fifty years, as more couples marry through church services or through a civil ceremony.

Finally, there is *polygamy*. Polygamy in Africa has been primarily polygyny, where the husband marries more than one wife. Outsiders seem to feel that it is *the* major characteristic of African family life, and believe that almost all marriages were or are polygynous. However, it is not the major characteristic of African family life, as recent estimates show, in fact, that for the following African countries, the number of polygynists per 100 married men ranges from 20.4 to 36.4: Benin, Chad, Congo, Gabon, Ghana, Kenya, Mali, Niger, Senegal, Tanzania, Togo and Zaire. In Burundi and Rwanda the number is even lower – 8.4 for both. The average number of wives is about two (Welch and Glick, 1981). As Welch and Glick have pointed out, the data are not necessarily suitable for generalizations since the quality of census information is poor and not available for concurrent time periods for all African countries. Yet those estimates do suggest that polygyny characterizes a minority of the African families.

Because polygyny had traditionally been a way of increasing family resources (Adepoju, 1977:142), it is likely to decline as the cost of educating children increases, and as polygyny proves too expensive in urban areas. We should be aware that work by Aryee (1978) suggests that a curvilinear trend rather than a simple decline represents the total picture over time, over many centuries. He argues that polygyny rates are lowest in more traditional and most modern groups in society, and highest among groups that are midway between modernity and tradition. Thus, we can impute from his data that polygyny may have historically increased when cash crops or other economic changes were introduced. Orubuloye (1981b) shows that this probably did occur at least among the Yoruba, where polygyny seems to have increased with the introduction of cocoa. More wives were needed to help in crop production, and wealthy farmers could afford more wives. He further suggests that polygyny will decrease in the future because of the expense of educating children.

Even though polygyny is on the decline in some parts of Africa, there is a possibility that extra-marital liaisons may be replacing formal marriages. Many men may be keeping women in towns without going through formal ceremonies and without informing the wife of these relationships. As Ware (1981) puts it, in West Africa, polygyny, both open and secret, is an ever-present possibility which influences family life regardless of the current marital type.

Clignet (1970) has listed these determinants of polygyny:

1) levirate;
2) imbalance in the sex ratio, with many men migrating out;
3) need to maintain a high birth rate;
4) complexity of female roles in African societies.

Of these determinants, the first and third are most convincing. A high birth rate was needed to ensure a large labour force in agricultural work. Recent work among the Yoruba women in Ibadan has shown that the fertility of women is largely unrelated to their type of marriage (Arowolo, 1981). This partly means that the individual women in plural unions do not have a lower fertility rate than women in monogamous unions. Hence, polygynous unions would have had, considering the offspring of all wives, more total children than monogamous unions. The imbalance in sex ratios may be a weak determinant since there are societies where imbalances in sex ratios do not exist, but where there is polygyny.

The nature of family life in polygynous unions differs somewhat in different ethnic groups, as this contrast between the Xhosa and the Nyakyusa shows (Wilson, 1977:192):

Xhosa	Nyakyusa
1 husband mediates among wives	1 mother-in-law mediates
2 husband allocates co-wives' work	2 mother-in-law allocates
3 co-wives are close	3 co-wives are not so close

Xhosa	**Nyakyusa**
4 conflict expressed through witchcraft	4 conflict expressed in other ways
5 elderly women cared for by daughters-in-law	5 elderly women do their own work
6 increase in status as women age	6 no increase

Overall, one could not conclude that polygyny is always the same. It is also true that the institution of polygyny has been carried over into settings where there is more strain and conflict than was normally the case. We must study both the traditional and modern variations of this institution before we can make any more definitive statements about it.

Methodological caution

As well as describing the African setting we should also describe the research setting, primarily the types of data collection from which African family studies have emerged. Most of the existing data were collected by anthropologists. Thus details on kinship terminology and the meaning of kin relationships are typical. There is also a lot of information on patterns of residence and inheritance. The basic data collection tools include key informant interviews, participant observation and genealogies. Many of the researchers tended to be non-indigenous scholars, although that has changed in the last twenty years.

In sociology, the studies tend to rely heavily on surveys, wherein a certain portion of the population is sampled and then interviewed. There are several problems with interviewing in the African environment. First of all, the interviewer may never be able to interview the interviewee privately. Relatives or neighbours often refuse to leave the scene of the interview, and the interview takes place under public scrutiny. Secondly, interviewing itself is so often irrelevant to people's pressing development needs that they may not try to give complete answers. Finally, the problems of different meaning between researchers and researched are compounded by problems of translation and by the common alien background of the foreign researcher. Thus, we should place highest reliability on family studies coming from indigenous researchers, but also read clearly to find out exactly how the study was carried out before we jump to unwarranted conclusions about African family life.

Finally, we suggest that more innovative techniques need to be used to study African families in the future. We need more time-budget studies in both urban and rural areas. Time-budget studies involve a description of how people use their time. Such time-budgets could tell us about the division of labour in the family, role conflicts and distribution of leisure time. Rather than trying for an unrealistic degree of privacy we may simply rely on group interviews where people can all answer questions together. For family conflict, more complete study needs to be undertaken of law court records dealing with divorce, child custody, inheritance, murder of spouses and so on. Records from psychiatric clinics should also be systematically analysed to assess family problems. Essays written by children about their family life would also be revealing, as we are finding in a study of child labour in East Africa. Life histories, as employed so effectively by Oscar Lewis, would also be quite innovative in African family research. More detailed studies of networks of friends and relatives which interrelate with families would also be creative if one followed the network linkages more closely by cross-checking information from other people in the network.

In general, we are saying that we need more creative methods to begin to fathom the intricacies of the African family. Mere agreement in typical responses or behaviour among people sampled in African nations or between African and non-African nations can be misleading. This outward agreement may be caused by methodological flaws. We thus need to be sure that what has been found out in research is a true reflection of African family life and that the meaning we attribute to certain facts is related to the way in which African family members would interpret the facts.

It will be desirable to provide a few definitions before we proceed to the main body of the work.

Terminology

There are a number of concepts which are basic to the rest of this book. The first concept is *family*. We begin by looking at the structural features of the family. A family at its simplest level includes a husband and a wife and their offspring. This is what is called a *nuclear family*. Recent changes in life styles have made it misleading to define a family as a husband and wife instead of a man and woman living together. Many couples live together and do indeed create a family in many societies without legal or traditional sanctions of this union. In fact, modern families have included only the original couple, with the couple refusing to separate even after finding themselves unable to have any children.

The reader should be alerted to the argument made by Murray (1981) in reference to the use of the nuclear family as the basic unit of analysis. His point is that the nuclear family may be a static type of measure which ignores changes in the family over time. What this means is that a nuclear family does exist in most cultures during particular stages in the family's life cycle, but other types of structure, such as the extended family, are also common during other stages. Over the life cycle, a family may change from nuclear to extended family form and back to nuclear again.

The structure of the family in terms of the numbers of individuals can be expanded in many ways. Children can grow up and start their own families and decide to live with their parents. Whenever the parents, their children and their children's children live together in one housing unit, this is referred to as an *extended family*. The term 'extended family' can also refer to families that include cousins of anyone in the nuclear family, or other relatives who are not nuclear family members. In the African setting, the household typically has relatives besides those of the nuclear family such as brothers of the father or mother. We also call a family extended if the ties with relatives outside the nuclear family are maintained through visiting or economic support.

In addition to the structure of the family we can also think about what is a family in terms of family *functions*. The functions can vary but normally include: reproduction, affection, socialization, economic cooperation and religious upbringing. When people argue that the family is disappearing they are usually referring to the loss of any of these functions of the family.

In societies like the kibbutzim, communal groups in Israel, parents do reproduce children, but are not responsible for socializing, the economic support or the religious education of their children. They are involved in giving their children affection only during their daily visits. All other functions are fulfilled by the communal caretakers in the nurseries and institutions for older children.

In Africa, the family is centred on reproduction of offspring more than any other function. Traditionally, socialization, affection and religious upbringing were matters for the larger kin group as well as the parents. More and more, socialization is now being taken over by educational institutions like schools and nurseries. Whereas in many rural areas, the family functions as a joint economic unit of production and consumption, this is rapidly changing. Husbands and wives often earn separate salaries today, and keep separate bank accounts. They arrange the household budget so that each spouse cares for selected items in the budget individually without a planned family budget.

The next concept we should consider is the *household*, which is often used alternatively with the term 'family' but is distinctive. We prefer Murray's (1981) definition of 'household' as being a unit of economic viability whether or not its members are physically dispersed at any one time. The *de jure* membership includes temporary absentees, while the *de facto* membership includes only persons actually resident in the village homestead at any one time. Such a definition is particularly appropriate since economic and political conditions often necessitate the physical separation of family members for years.

Marriage is a union between two people of the opposite sex, which is institutionalized by the payment of bridewealth or by religious or civil ceremonies. The parties are entitled to certain rights and have responsibilities to each other. The marriage is meant primarily for the creation of children, though other marriages are meant to consolidate wealth, create security over property or provide companionship for the couple. In Africa, companionship has only recently become a major reason for marriages, especially in urban areas, where partners often select their own spouse. Most marriages were arranged by parents, and even today most children seek permission for marriage to the person of their choice.

Bridewealth was the payment which was given to finalize the customary marriage. It was given only after all preliminary stages were completed. First, a visit had to be made to the parents to ask for the daughter to be given in marriage. Gifts were given as a variety of informal meetings later ensued. At those meetings the amount of the bridewealth was agreed upon. Bridewealth guaranteed the husband's right over the offspring of the union, and thus is more common in patrilineal societies. It stabilized marriages since the couple was urged to stay together as relatives helped them sort out their problems. A marriage break-up meant the return of the bridewealth to the husband. This was often very difficult since the bridewealth had often been reinvested in other forms, such as in payments for other bridewealth, and was thus hard to retrieve.

'Bridewealth' is preferred to the term 'brideprice' since, after long academic controversies, it was felt that brideprice carried a connotation of purchasing the wife which was not a true reflection of this social custom. Bridewealth did compensate the parents for the loss of their daughter, but it was not meant to be an assessment of her 'cost' in cattle and goods. Today, the custom has become closer to a brideprice since parents, imbued with economic values, have begun to calculate the worth of their daughters in monetary terms. Higher levels of education lead to a larger bridewealth payment, until the college-educated woman becomes too expensive for men of her age who are not wealthy. When bridewealth becomes unreasonably high and becomes a way of measuring the value of the woman, it is changing from bridewealth to brideprice. When bridewealth changes from being a way of committing two families to uphold the marriage and becomes a way to acquire quick wealth, the social utility of bridewealth changes. It no longer makes marriages stable and seldom guarantees absolute rights over offspring even in customary marriages.

A closely related term is 'dowry', which is a gift to the woman to be married, not to her family. It is given by the parents of the woman. It is rare in Africa but is more likely to occur among matrilineal groups.

The term *matrilineal* means that descent is traced through the female line, usually the mother, while in patrilineal systems descent is traced through the male line. This has importance for inheritance of property, rights of children and rights of parents over children. There are systems where descent is traced through both mother and father, these being called 'bilineal'.

The term *matriarchal* is often confused with matrilineal. However, matriarchal refers to the rule of women or mothers. Women do not necessarily rule in the political sphere simply because inheritance is traced through them. At the household level, a family may be referred to as matriarchal if the mother's authority is much greater than the father's. Patriarchal refers to the rule of fathers or the dominance of fathers in the family authority system.

Residence patterns of the married couple are important in determining the influence of the extended family members on the life of the couple and the degree of economic independence or dependence of the couple in relationship to the extended family. In patrilocal systems, the couple establish residence near the husband's family; in matrilocal systems, residence is near the mother's family. Patrilocal residence is often associated with patrilineal inheritance systems, though there are many variations. Among other groups, such as the Baganda, the place of residence is not near either the husband's or wife's family and is called 'neolocal'.

Single-parent family refers to a family with only one parent and one or more children. These children may be the natural children of the parent or fostered or adopted in some way. The parent may be separated, divorced, widowed or unmarried. Unmarried single parents are usually women in Africa, as it common elsewhere. Males who have children out of wedlock and are not living with the mother of the child usually marry a woman who will agree to take care of these children or take the children to their parents or brothers who will then raise the children. Unmarried mothers are becoming more common in Africa today. Traditionally, women who gave birth to illegitimate children were either forced to get married, especially to an older man with other wives as a type of punishment, or were physically beaten. The woman was also in some communities banished from the village or would run away to live elsewhere to escape the wrath of the villagers. Thus unmarried mothers were almost unheard of.

Unmarried mothers in Africa are today the ones most responsible for abandoned babies, left along roads or in bushes; or the dumping of children into toilets or rubbish bins. Many other unmarried mothers leave the children to be raised by their own parents, or leave the child or children with the father to raise them in whatever way he is able. The majority of unmarried mothers are, however, forced to leave school and stay with their parents to raise the child.

The households with female single-parent heads are usually called *female-headed households*. In economic terms this merely means that the woman is the main income earner in the family and the one responsible for the financial management of the household. Estimates of female-headed households are up to 30 per cent in some parts of Africa especially towns (Clark, 1982). In rural areas, female-headed households are largely those wherein the husband has lived away for years, working in towns, and seldom returns home or supports the family. In urban areas, the female-headed household is usually the result of divorce or widowhood. These female-headed households tend to have more financial problems, and more trouble in socializing children because there is only one parent.

There may also be *irregular unions* which closely resemble formal marriages. They differ from marriages in that they are of shorter duration in most cases and are not institutionalized by any ceremonies or payment of bridewealth. Cohabitation, 'living together', or common law marriages are all irregular unions and mean about the same thing. A common law marriage is a form of cohabitation in which the man and woman have lived together for years and are recognised as husband and wife by friends and/or relatives.

A practice has arisen whereby a married man 'keeps' a woman outside his marital home, by paying for her house and other expenses. This practice is becoming an alternative to contracting another marriage. The wife seldom knows about the 'kept' wife and the 'kept' wife has few legal rights stemming from this union.

Parkin (1973) differentiates temporary or irregular urban unions in Kampala in terms of three dimensions:

1) whether the union is arranged in towns or rural areas;
2) whether the union is intra- or inter-tribal; and
3) whether the wife is considered permanent or temporary.

Men will often cohabit with women of one ethnic group but marry women of their own or a closely related ethnic group. While the centralized tribes such as the Toro and Ganda do not condemn mixed unions, the uncentralized groups such as the Lango and Teso oppose such unions, fearing that bridewealth may not be returned if the wife is barren. Among the Toro and Ganda, no bridewealth is recoverable. Parkin also argues that the uncentralized ethnic groups have more strict control over the activities of their female kin so that few are allowed to move to and live freely in towns.

Finally, we may briefly deal with concubinage. Muslims were allowed to keep concubines, who were women who lived with the husband, often in the same compound as his wife. They had well-defined rights and duties, but were often purchased as one would purchase a slave. Stroebel (1979) indicates that such a woman could not be sold during the lifetime of her master and she would be free when the master died if she had given birth to a child of his. In 1907, in the Mombasa area, slavery was abolished but not concubinage, and in 1909 the ordinance abolishing slavery was amended to include financial obligations for concubines. Concubines were not wives in that they were never formally married, but they and their children did have certain rights of inheritance.

We now turn to the main body of the work, beginning with the internal functioning of the African family.

2   Internal processes of the family

In this chapter, we examine the internal functioning of the family under four headings: stages in the family life cycle; the family and socialization; the family and the division of labour; and family power structures and processes.

Stages in the family life cycle

Stages in the family life cycle are used to describe the ageing of a family group from its birth at marriage to the death of the family unit. Stages are typically described in terms of a nuclear family model, and are characterized by both the size of the family and the ages of the members. At every stage, the family changes, so that the division of labour, the family budget and the needs and problems of the family are very distinctive. Any attempts to introduce social change to the family or to engage the participation of family members in community projects should take stages in the life cycle into consideration. Marriage counselling must also operate from a knowledge of the stage of development of the family.

Life-cycle stages are partially related to the African age-grade system. As individuals advance in age, they enter different age grades. Ceremonial events highlight the changes in roles and rights as individuals grow older (Gulliver, 1963). In the past individuals married only when they had reached a certain age grade. Just as responsibilities decreased as people entered old age, so the family life cycle involved variation in duties depending upon the age, size and development of the family. The first stage in a nuclear family, before there are children, contains only a married couple. At this stage the couple may be very cooperative in the division of labour and in decision-making. When children are born, the family is in a second stage where responsibilities increase for the women in terms of household and child-care duties. Husbands may be overburdened with work, trying to keep up with financial responsibilities. As children get older and are able to help in family work, the family enters the next stage. Older children help but may also begin to take part in the family's decision-making process, especially if they are males. Children eventually either leave their original family or bring their spouses to stay with the original family, this step initiating another stage. Finally, when one of the original spouses dies, or the couple divorces, the family is, in a way, 'dying'.

Of course, these are stages in the life cycle of a typical nuclear family.

These stages differ, depending upon whether children are actually born to the couple, and whether the marriage is monogamous or polygamous. If children are not born, a husband in the traditional system had a right to take another wife. In a manner of speaking, the first wife and her husband are in the stage of their marriage which will last until one of them dies or remarries. Nothing will greatly change in their relationship over the years because children are not part of this family. As the couple gets older their individual ageing processes alone will alter their relationship only slightly.

When the marriage is polygamous, the husband is usually at a different stage with each of his wives. This means that the critical stages are spread over time rather than happening concurrently. For instance, payment of school fees for children from each wife are spread over many years rather than concentrated within a few years. Today, however, men who obtain outside work can often get several wives quite early, and thus the stages may be concurrent for all families. Each wife then tends to be individually responsible for her own children.

The original family breaks up with the death of the husband, unless an older son rather quickly takes over as head of the household. Among the Sonjo, the father retains control over the family land until he dies. Winans (1964) summarizes the typical sequence of events when the father retains control over the land until his death. He says that various factors

> . . .will often prolong clustering of dependent or semi-dependent men and their families around a senior man. The situation will ultimately end, however, with the final marriage of the youngest man, the death of the *pater*, and the final settlement of inheritance.

However, among some groups like the Arusha, sons are given portions of the family estate as soon as they acquire families of their own (Gray and Gulliver, 1964:5).

When a man has died leaving a young wife with small children, this woman is likely to be married in a levirate union to one of his brothers. In this type of union the marriage continues, in a way, even with the death of the husband, since the woman's children are the children of the late husband even if fathered by her husband's brother. The important point is that the family does not always dissolve on the death of the husband.

The stages can also be delayed or brought forward by intentional manipulation of individuals. For example, although a couple should, by most cultural norms, be married first and then have children, many couples now have a child or children first and then get married. This is largely due to the fact that it is difficult to dissolve civil or Christian marriages if a woman does not bear a child. Hence, waiting until she bears a child seems to some couples to provide a type of surety that the marriage will be a stable one.

The departure of the children from the family of birth is often delayed because of lack of bridewealth money. Sons, specifically, must often wait until their sisters' marriages provide bridewealth which can then be used by the brothers to obtain wives. Younger daughters are often made to wait for their own marriages until older daughters are married.

African parents may also need their children to stay at home longer if their children's labour is vital to the family production system and if hired labour is not available for one reason or another. Chayanov summarizes the relevance of the life cycle of the family to labour in this way:

> Every family, depending on its age, is in its different phases of development a completely distinct labour machine as regards labour force, intensity of demand, consumer–worker ratio, and the possibilities of applying the principle of complex cooperation (Chayanov, 1966:60).

Thus, when rural African children are most able to contribute substantial amounts of labour, parents may prolong the departure of these children. One could also argue, using Chayanov's description, that when rural parents decide to have large families, they are thinking more about the 'productive' stage of the life cycle when children produce more than they consume rather than about the early stages when children may be more of a burden than an asset. These parents then behave very rationally by anticipation of future stages in the family's life cycle.

We can also look at the life cycle of the family in terms of the effect that it can have on the status of members within the family. Muslim women are isolated and submissive in their young married life. When these women are older they become very powerful, since they alone can see the face of the potential bride-to-be for their sons. They are also the only ones who are able to talk intimately with the bride-to-be to discover whether she is suitable to become a wife of her son. Judith Brown (1982) lists a variety of ways by which African mothers become advantaged as they grow older:

1) if there are grown daughters, the daughters do the work around the house (Acholi women);
2) the older woman (in Burundi) has the right to overwork her daughter-in-law, or even to have her sent away;
3) there are expanded opportunities for achievement and recognition in ritual activities, in medicine, religion, and classification of kin groups (among the Bemba, and !Kung).

Men also gain in status over time. However, we are not dealing here with a simple process whereby ageing alone earns people respect, but rather with one in which the combination of old age and having children determines the increase in respect and power given to individuals.

In their old age, African parents are supposed to be taken care of by their children. Thus, the stage after children have left home should be a happy one. Although they are becoming physically incapacitated, the increased respect and the assistance of children make this stage easier in some respects.

Finally, there comes the dissolution of the original family unit. When one spouse dies, the other may be taken to live with one of the sons, especially if the remaining spouse is not able to care for his or her own needs. Divorce is another way in which marriages are dissolved. In traditional systems the divorce resulted in the woman returning to her family and, depending upon the circumstances, a large portion of the bridewealth being returned. The children would normally stay with the mother until they were a bit older, then they would go to live with the father, at least in patrilineal systems.

Reasons for divorce as shown in a study in Cameroon include the following:

1) ill treatment of wife by the husband;
2) marriage forced by parents against their daughter's wish;
3) extensive neglect of wife by husband;
4) marriage of a husband to a second wife;
5) the husband was a Muslim and the parents did not like him;
6) the wife delivered the child in the hospital and had it baptized;
7) the wife's parents hated the husband;
8) the mother-in-law quarrelled with the wife a lot;
9) the husband wanted sexual relations when their baby was only three months old;
10) one of the children died suddenly and people blamed the wife;
11) the husband threatened to kill the wife;
12) the husband sold the cassava farm without wife's permission;
13) the husband had too many wives and did not care for one wife's children;
14) the husband refused to help clear the farm or buy oil, salt or clothes;
15) the husband gave the only daughter in marriage to an old man;
16) the wife was having recurrent abortions (Lantum, 1979).

Divorce seems to have been more peaceful and less disturbing to the spouses and children in traditional African systems. Currently, however, divorce is highly disruptive since many people use the courts to fight over children and over property. Uncertainties over legal rights and conflicting normative systems make such fights more common today.

Another way in which we can describe the internal functioning of the family is through the process of socialization.

The family and socialization

Perhaps the most striking characterization of socialization in the African family is the large number of agents of socialization, as opposed to family systems where only the parents are involved in socialization of their own children. In this section, we will compare traditional and modern African families. Traditional practices still continue in many rural areas, so we use both the present and past tense in the discussion. Within modern families, there may also be differences among the various socio-economic classes.

Traditionally, a child was socialized by the whole community in the sense that he could be corrected or disciplined by any adult if he misbehaved. Adults also had full authority to tell any child to perform simple duties, although this authority was not normally abused. If children did not act properly or were disrespectful towards adults, the parents would be blamed but only to a limited extent.

Age groups or peer groups were perhaps the most important socializing agents. They were usually sex-segregated. They supported parental values and duties to the larger kin and ethnic group. Peer groups are similarly important in most societies, but differ in their degree of control over socialization and in their support of parental values. Like modern American peer groups, traditional African peer groups had a great deal of control over young people's behaviour. Differences exist in terms of support of parental values and the period of life during which the groups influence individual behaviour. Traditional African peer groups, unlike modern American peer groups, were pro-parental in terms of the values they accepted, and exerted control throughout life. Finally, comparing these peer groups with Israeli kibbutzim (settlements where children are reared communally) and Soviet peer groups, African peer groups were more concerned with maintenance of the family or kin values than with larger institutional or national values. In other words, the peer groups in traditional African society worked in conjunction with parental and kin discipline. This is the opposite to the Israeli kibbutzim, where parents are never supposed to discipline their children since discipline is the duty of the communal caretakers. There is also a contrast with the Soviet system as it operated in the 1950s, where peer groups were expected to exercise much more control over children than their parents.

African peer groups disciplined members primarily through social ostracism, which consisted of open disapproval of bad behaviour and continuous rebukes until the behaviour ceased. These peer groups also refused to talk to or interact with deviant members. In other, rarer instances, physical punishment was used. These groups were especially important in ensuring the upholding of sexual codes of behaviour. Violators of such codes were reported to the peer groups, and if, for instance, the violator was a young man, he would lose his right of meeting and interacting with young women for some time.

Grandparents were other important agents of socialization in traditional African society. They were instrumental in introducing young people to more sensitive topics such as husband–wife relationships and sexual behaviour, as well as the larger societal roles, values and traditions. They relied largely on story-telling, proverbs and songs as techniques of socialization. After the age of ten or so, grandmothers were more closely involved with female grandchildren and grandfathers with male grandchildren.

Lastly, it should be noted that siblings were very heavily involved in the socialization process of younger siblings. Elder siblings sometimes had authority equivalent to the authority of their parents over the young children. The elder siblings were highly respected by their younger brothers and sisters, and were expected to sacrifice for the younger ones as if they were their own children. Much of this type of responsibility has been carried over to the modern times with older children being expected to put the other children through school if the older ones obtain employment.

Fostering was traditionally and still is a common feature of African family life. Children are often fostered by adult relatives who have no children. In this case, the child provides company and help for those who would otherwise be alone. However, there is also fostering in the form of exchange of children, say between married brothers each taking one or more children from the other. These fostered children all know their real parents, but spend much of their life away from their biological parents. They often call both their uncle and aunt and their real parents 'father' or 'mother'.

Although there may be hidden psychological costs for the child in such fostering arrangements, no research has been done on this aspect. Hence, we can only imagine the situation. Outwardly, there are certainly fewer references to real biological relationships than might occur in other cultures. Openly, hardly any reference is made to the foster children as less than 'real' members of the family. In fact, these children may actually be treated more kindly than the parents' own children although discipline is likely to be maintained equally for all children.

An obvious result of such fostering is that the foster child is less emotionally attached to the real parents although he may be just as detached from the foster parents. There is also a possibility that the foster child may subtly try to attain a special status in the family through academic or sports achievements in order to compensate for having been sent to live elsewhere by his parents.

Esther Goody has made the most comprehensive analysis of the types and functions of African family fostering. From her work, one could perhaps argue that in West Africa parents foster children only when the potential foster parents can offer the children special educational training or job opportunities. In East Africa, however, it seems that most fostering is done to re-emphasize kin solidarity – meaning that each child is a child not only for the parents but the larger kin group. In both West and East Africa, children are still sent to childless relatives as helpers, though this practice is rapidly diminishing in importance in some places where schooling becomes more significant than children's labour contributions.

It should also be emphasized that the typical European attitude of parents that the child is 'theirs' is not so common among traditional African parents, at least as reflected in overt behaviour. We have mentioned that outwardly the real and foster children are not treated any differently in daily interaction. Real parents may visit the child from time to time but may never insist on dictating where the child goes to school, when (or even if) the child should visit the parents' home, even in cases where the child is to be away most of his childhood. The real parents may also not openly try to make the child aware of who his biological siblings are, with the result that the children usually refer to each other as brother or sister, not cousins, and truly think of themselves as such. When such foster children are old enough to marry, the foster parents are often just as deeply involved in the marriage activities, especially giving consent, as the real parents. When the foster child starts working they may show only slight favour to the real parents since they have developed strong emotional bonds with the foster parents.

There are and were cases of fostering non-relatives' children. Such foster children are not as fortunate as those who are fostered by relatives. They are forever reminded of their position, and are often overworked compared to the other children in the household. This fostering is a result of poverty. Parents give their children to another family, hoping that the child will have a chance for a better life. This chance may never actually materialize. Such children may be physically and sexually abused by adults in the household and may in their adulthood become abusers. Other children in the household may treat the foster children as outcasts or servants, adding to the foster children's psychological burdens.

So far, the parents have been bypassed in this discussion, because they were in fact only one of many agents of socialization in traditional African society. We have considered them last to emphasize this fact. Parents were most directly involved in socializing their children into adult roles, particularly their roles within the family division of labour. After the age of 8 or 10, most children learned their appropriate work roles by labouring beside the parent of the same sex. Hence, boys spent more work hours beside the father and girls more time with the mother. The children thus learned their future adult roles through actual performance of many of these roles from an early age.

Performing certain work roles was not only intended to teach the child particular skills or technical perfection in that work; it was also meant to make the child diligent, persistent and responsible to all others. In other words, character-moulding was a central aim of parental socialization efforts.

Parents were more likely than other agents to use physical punishment. Beatings were usually given by fathers, though in polygamous households the mothers were more involved in physically disciplining children. Parents also refused children food if they misbehaved. Discipline was harshest in the cultures where there was a very clear structural hierarchy, in terms of having royal families, or extreme status differences between sexes. Fathers seemed to have been more authoritarian and strict in disciplining in cultures where the men were accorded very special respect and forms of deference, and were privileged in terms of diet and leisure time, such as among the Baganda.

In modern African family life, some traditional practices such as fostering are still carried out, though with less frequency. The authority of older children over younger ones is also continued, though in fewer households than before. New agents of socialization have entered family life – the houseworkers. When the modern African woman enters wage labour, she needs someone to care for her very young children while she works. Houseworkers have been known to become very powerful keeping the children in silence through their ability to threaten and coerce the children. Children may spend more time with the house workers than the mother or father, and may at times see the mother as an unreasonable disciplinarian and the nurse/nanny as a kindly woman. Such a nurse may have worked on the children's minds very subtly, offering special favours so that she is protected from any harmful revelation by the children to the parents.

More often, there is no intention to compete with the authority of the parents. The problem may simply be that the houseworker has such a different educational and home background from that of the employer that she inadvertently presents an alternative moral and value system to that of the parents. In towns, houseworkers are often from different linguistic communities from the parents. This means that either the child learns the worker's language or the worker must stumble along with the child's language, often introducing major flaws in grammar and pronunciation. We should remember that language is not a neutral tool of socialization. There is in fact mounting evidence from Bernstein (1977) and his followers that language differs according to class in ways that limit a child's ability to succeed in school. Houseservants, then, are major socializers of the children in terms of language and moral behaviour.

While not expecting all houseservants to be moral deviants, one should realize that parents have less control over such servants in the sense that the servants are often strangers with no moral obligation to the parents. If they are also poorly paid they may revenge themselves by taking a deeper hold on the children. A different situation exists where houseservants are relatives. They socialize the children and do other work for the family but are answerable to the larger kin group for their actions. They may feel that their position in the family is a respected one, and thus feel obliged to socialize children into obedience and love for the parents.

In modern times and places, the role of fathers as agents of socialization has altered tremendously. They seldom work beside their children, and expect the mother to administer most discipline because of their absence from home during the day. Some fathers, on the other hand, spend more time with their children and have become more affectionate towards them than their own fathers were with them.

Grandparental roles in socialization have been severely circumscribed in urban areas because of physical distance between the village and the town and because of difficulties where the extended family lives as a residential unit in the town. Peer-group roles in modern times have been altered as well. Peer groups are still strong agents in a child's socialization. However, in modern times they are less supportive of the values of their parents or the larger cultural group.

Where there are illegitimate grandchildren, however, more and more grandparents are raising them until their own children are capable of doing so. Unfortunately, the kindness of the grandparents has led to an increase in the rates of illegitimacy even in rural areas, as young people no longer worry seriously about the care of such children. Grandparents, in fact, tend to spoil these children; indeed, it is hard to imagine a grandparent disciplining and socializing a grandchild in the way in which he socialized his own children.

In many other countries, socialization techniques have differed from one social class to another, with poorer parents being more likely to use physical punishment than wealthier parents. Wealthier parents tend to reason more with their children, use more withdrawal of love and more rewards in socializing their children. On the basis of a few studies, it appears that class has had a similar influence in Africa. Levine and others (1967) tell us that traditional fathers in Ibadan emphasize obedience, submission and respect from their children, whereas modern fathers stress personal responsibility, individual autonomy and social equality for their children. The difference is that there is no evidence of a shift from physical punishment to psychological techniques, as has occurred in the United States, Britain and some European countries. Gamble (1963) showed that the father's type of occupation determines the type of socialization in a mining town in Sierra Leone.

Clignet (1967) reported that for the urban Bété, where the majority of husbands are manual workers, the parents prefer to have their children reared by other kin, and there is more cooperation among co-wives in socializing children and more emphasis on physical punishment. In comparison, for the largely white-collar Abouré, parents are more likely to raise their own children, and there is less cooperation among co-wives in raising children and use of physical punishment. There are certainly other differences among classes in child-rearing, but these studies highlight some of the more important differences.

Let us now consider the division of labour in the family.

The family and the division of labour

Pre-colonial patterns

In the pre-colonial period, the family division of labour was less conflict-ridden than in later times. Female and male roles, older and young people's roles were accepted largely without question since such roles were seen as 'natural', supported by the ethnic myths of origin. Women were mainly responsible for the home, food-crop production and the care of children. In West Africa, women were also involved in trading activities, which somewhat reduced the amount of time they could spend in their other roles. Men were usually responsible for protecting the home, for hunting and caring for cattle. Among many groups, the men did the harder physical work like clearing fields, and tended to the more permanent food crops like bananas and yams. There is a great deal of variation among ethnic groups with regard to the building of houses, making of cloth, basketry and pottery-making. Within any one group, each of these activities was restricted to one sex and, according to many traditional beliefs, misfortunes would befall any adult who attempted to do the work of another sex.

Children began helping at very early ages. They were not overworked but were expected to contribute through performance of tasks geared to their age and sex. Before the age of eight to ten years, there was little sexual differentiation in the duties given to children, tasks being sexually differentiated after that period. Children learned persistence, cooperation and many other values in addition to the skill in performing a task. By the age of seven, most children were capable of caring for younger siblings while the mother did other work like farming or trading.

Polygamous families usually functioned as separate households in terms of the division of labour, with several exceptions. In most of these families, the women each had their own plot of land, which was farmed by the woman herself and her children. Each woman may have been required to bring a meal to her husband every day or on an appointed day. Each wife was thus responsible for feeding her children and providing food for the husband. Although the women normally did not assist each other in farming, exceptions did occur. When a wife had just delivered or had fallen sick, the other wives might assist her in her work for a short period.

It is also known that a wife may have asked her husband to get another wife if she found the work too much. Younger wives may have been allocated more and harder work if the power of the senior wife or wives was great. It appears that while many tasks – like grinding of grain and clothing preparation – may have been done collectively by all the wives, many other duties – like cooking and farming – were done separately.

The larger family unit and neighbours were also very important in that each family could expect assistance from others in periods of work peaks, such as harvest periods or for major efforts like constructing a granary.

Colonial patterns

The imposition of colonial rule led to a variety of changes in the division of family labour. Although the impact was not uniform for all ethnic groups, even in one country, changes were quite similar for many ethnic groups on the continent.

The introduction of forced labour and a cash economy were perhaps the most disruptive types of changes. As a result of forced labour men were often withdrawn from the villages for long periods of time, during which the women and children attempted to fulfil the father's roles. In later periods, there were cases of women and children being forced into labour, leaving the village homesteads largely unattended for much of the year. Migration of men outside the village led to similar results, with the family's roles being primarily undertaken by the wife and children. Even when men did return home, their overall authority over the division of labour must have weakened considerably because of the wife's experience in running the household independently.

Children were drawn into exploitive non-family labour for the first time. They worked on plantations, in the mines and as farm and house workers. While international regulations were being formulated to eliminate non-family child labour in the early 1900s, children in African countries under colonial rule were often competitors with their parents for jobs. During periods of political upheaval, when fathers were incarcerated, children in places like Kenya helped save the tea harvest or otherwise filled a gap in the labour force.

Parental authority over children declined during this period because of a multitude of changes. When this authority declined, the children's attitudes about their participation were likely to have become more negative, seeing home tasks more and more as an unwanted burden

Working for parents may have been deeply resented and thus the potential educative value to the child was reduced. One of the reasons for the decline in parental authority was the introduction of schools and churches, both of which offered alternative systems of values, as well as new sources of authority. Closely allied to this was the moral degradation associated with racial discrimination, which reduced parents' dignity and thus often children's respect for their parents. Fanon's work deals with this type of psychological impact of colonialism. New cultural values, associated with being a British or French 'gentleman' or 'lady' also had their effect. Working with hands became debasing so that even after political independence, school leavers refused farm work as being below their dignity. The proper gentleman or lady had servants to perform the duties in the household for the family. African women, in fact, often had their only access to towns through work as maids or nurses for the British or French settlers or administrators.

In general, a whole new set of cultural values and a new economic-political system created severe disruptions for many ethnic groups. Traditional patterns of division of labour were increasingly questioned as a result of potent forces of change.

Current roles

Many of the changes initiated in the colonial period have continued to affect family roles to an even greater degree. Longer periods of schooling have reduced the hours that children have available for helping at home. However, in rural areas, children still help after school hours and during vacation periods. Female children are often more burdened by after-school duties than male children because the after-school duties are largely female ones and because a female child's school performance may not be as highly valued as that of a male child. Thus, while the male child is seen as needing time to do homework, homework may seem to parents to be of secondary importance for the female child. For both sexes, their contribution to the family usually continues well after they leave the household, though males have a heavier obligation. Money or other types of assistance is usually given to parents once the child begins some type of wage labour, and this continues even after he is married. Children in towns spend very little time helping at home unlike their rural counterparts. These town children do, however, have an obligation to help their parents if their parents are not financially well off.

Husband and wife roles are changing in both rural and urban areas. In rural areas in most parts of the continent, women still tend to be responsible for the home, children and subsistence farming. Husbands seem to have control over the cash crops although the wife and children may provide most of the labour for the crops. This is especially the case when school vacations correspond to cash-crop harvest periods. Women are not always acquiescent in providing labour for which they may get no visible returns, and conflicts may result when the husband's use of the money is not acceptable to the family.

Women in rural areas may also have new roles which result in less time for traditional ones. Self-help activities and women's groups are examples, where being a leader or a member gives a woman a new role with a requisite demand on her time and energies. Husbands may still expect the traditional roles of a wife to be fulfilled as they always have been. Arguments may ensue when the husband's and wife's expectations about each other's roles do not agree.

In urban areas, conflicts are worse since women often have full-time jobs. They may return from work, and start all over again helping children with school work, cooking and mending clothes. If they are teachers, they may not start preparations for lessons until after all the children have gone to sleep. It seems that urban women are under a great deal of strain trying to manage a full-time job and much of the housework. However, much depends on the economic resources of the family, since servants are very common in middle and higher income families. Even with servants, the woman must learn to manage them properly, and may have many problems if these people are inexperienced or irresponsible especially in child care. The wife may even have to be absent frequently from work, taking children to doctors or standing in for missing house servants.

Husbands tend to spend more time with friends and in leisure activities than in helping at home after work. Their attendance at work is less likely to be interrupted by household crises, and they thus are seen as more 'stable' workers. Few husbands help much with the children's homework and they may seldom feel pressure from having too many demanding roles. Some may in fact feel that their only role is to provide money for the family's maintenance. Even then, after the wife has worked for some time, her husband may drastically reduce his economic contribution, expecting his wife to use her wages for household needs, making his family role minimal indeed.

Family power structures and processes

In general family theory, family power processes include both power and authority. Whereas power refers to one's ability to change or exploit the behaviour of others, authority is one type of power which is based on norms which clearly legitimize a person's position and requires that deference and respect be accorded that person. People may also derive power from control over economic resources rather than norms.

In this section, we have decided to deal with power processes in terms of two closely related topics: decision-making and authority structures. Although these are not the only two components of family power systems, they are the ones for which there are some data on African families. Authority structures here refer to the types of leadership positions in the family and the types of resources from which the power in the family derives. Decision-making and conflict management are two specific modes of interaction or processes whereby power is exercised in the family. (Conflict management is dealt with later in the book.)

The most comprehensive review of family power structure is Scanzoni's (1979) article, in which he attempts to analyse family power as it would be interpreted in any other social institution, rather than seeing family processes as set apart from power as manifested in other political or economic spheres. This attempt is particularly welcome when, as now, those women's rights which are being emphasized through the United Nations Decade of Women (1975–1985) are economic, political and social rights.

In families, the typical positions of authority include the normative 'head', the emotional leader, the supporter and the expert. All of these positions derive from somewhat different resources. The normative head is usually the father, his position being given to him by African tradition. Thus even if the father is unemployed, he is still respected and deferred to in most families. As head, the father was walked behind, or knelt down to or served the best food. In reality this normative position was strongly related to the head's control over land, inheritance and traditional rites. When the control over these other resources is lost, the normative reinforcement may also decline until the person loses authority.

The emotional leader was often the mother, since she was closer to the children from birth and was supposed to keep a 'happy home'. Unlike the Parsonian position, which holds that the emotional or expressive role is held by one person in the family to the exclusion of other roles (Zelditch, 1956), recent research work has shown how misleading that is since African women were and in many cases still are also supporters (the so-called 'instrumental' leader of Parsons and Bales) (Crano and Aronoff, 1975). The supporter provided the resources to sustain the family's functioning, such as food, clothing and shelter. The expert is someone who is literate in a family of illiterates, or one who is old and knows the clan history, or one who can recite all the prayers from very long texts. Respect is given to such members because of their special skill, although these skills may also create family conflict if used improperly in family circles. More and more younger people are using their education as a weapon against their uneducated parents.

In addition to these general positions in every family authority is related to the matrilineal/patrilineal distinctions. Clignet (1970) showed that the matrilineal Abouré women had more power in the family than the women among the patrilineal Bété. Divorce rates tend to be higher in matrilineal societies since women do not lose much through divorce, neither the land nor the children. Matriliny is a form of

> ... political economy which minimizes individual male control over power and resources, guarantees women's control over offspring, land and remittances from adult children (Poewe, 1978:364).

Poewe notes that there is a great deal of antagonism between the sexes over the matrilineal system, the reason being that men want to have more control over resources, particularly the inheritance of land. Unlike patrilineal societies, men in the Luapula (Zambia) matrilineal group must confess sexual transgressions to the wife's mother if the wife has difficulty in childbirth. Repeated difficulty in childbirth gives the woman the right to divorce her husband.

Furthermore, unlike patrilineal systems where the wife comes to live in her husband's place, in matrilineal systems the wife may or may not live in the same place as her husband. The Abouré women, for example, visit their husbands but live separately most of the time; their husbands are not supposed to visit them in their house. This gives the woman more independence and control.

In terms of the process of decision-making, sociologists have differentiated three modes of decision-making in terms of the degree of collaboration between husband and wife. First, there is the syncratic mode, whereby the husband and wife have joint discussions on the same issues; second, there is the autonomous mode, whereby each make decisions separately about different issues; and last, the autocratic mode, in which one party dictates decisions to the other (Herbst, 1952). Oppong's (1981) study is the most comprehensive one yet published on decision-making in modern African families. Dealing with a matrilineal, middle-class group in Ghana, she shows in case studies of specific families how decision-making is closely related to the degree of sharing of tasks in the division of labour in the family and the extent to which husbands were linked to kin members through financial support or ownership of property. The syncratic families in her study were relatively isolated from neighbours, associates and relatives; and the husband and wife shared a variety of chores. The couples with an autonomous relationship had few joint budgeting arrangements, and 'nearly all had many activities and interests distracting their attention from the home' (Oppong, 1981:134). Both husband and wife tended to maintain close contact with their own kin, usually visited these kin alone and had equivalent resources. These couples did not share chores in the house and tended to be critical of each other's behaviour. Finally, the autocratic households were husband-dominated, the husband had command over greater resources, the couple had complementary roles, and the husband had close contact with many friends and relatives. The wives had heavy responsibilities in the house, and the husbands tended to discourage outside employment by the wife.

We must comment further about modern family budgeting. Household budgeting arrangements are often the result of a puzzling process of decision-making since there is seldom any clear-cut way in which decisions are made in many African families. If the wife works in some type of wage employment, the wife often takes over all the costs for household supplies, wages for houseservants and perhaps even children's school uniforms. Although the husband may ask her where her money has gone if she runs short, she is not allowed to ask him where his money has gone. They often keep separate bank accounts and seldom consult each other about purchases. The only time there is a semblance of joint decision-making is when there is a crisis such as a lack of money for school fees. Then the two may decide who pays what or where they can get the needed money for fees, without really telling each other honestly how much money each has saved. The husband may purchase a car only to come and tell his wife afterwards that he thinks he *will* buy such and such a type of car. The salary of the husband may be spent on contributions to relatives or building houses or buying land in the village, without his wife knowing any of these facts. If she knew, she would disagree with such expenditures. Whereas the husband's salary is also easily used to buy beer or food for friends, the wife's salary is meant to be spent on the household. Once the couple agree to pay for items like utilities or food, that pattern tends to stay, regardless of the differential increases that may occur for any item because there is little discussion about such matters. Thus, imbalances are likely to occur, with resultant arguments. When one party purchases an item such as funiture, the other may show resentment that the money was spent in that way since there is seldom prior agreement. When there is money saved, it is quickly spent since there is no mutual plan for the use of saved money. Thus, the whole process could be described as puzzling, since decisions are seldom made by the couple together but rather are made independently, often secretly, and then presented as a *fait accompli*.

As argued by writers elsewhere in the world under what is called 'resource theory' (Scanzoni, 1979), originally formulated by Blood and Wolfe, Oppong's work shows that the resources of the husband and wife largely determine their relative power in decision-making and their influence over domestic organization (Oppong, 1981:122). In addition to resources, networks of kin members and friends were important in that they would exert influence on the couple's decision-making. Sharing of chores or tasks indicates a willingness to cooperate in all spheres of domestic life, especially decision-making. Sharing of tasks also increases mutual respect, which is vital to open communication.

Clignet identified other factors which influence African familial power:

1) type of descent system;
2) functionality of the domestic role allocated to women;
3) degree of economic independence of women;
4) changes of residence, especially to urban environments;
5) features of the polygynous family (Clignet, 1970:35).

The second factor refers to the number and significance of the wife's contributions, such as the number of children she has borne, the extent to which she shares in the husband's business enterprises and the degree to which she is responsible for the socialization of the children. Economic independence means the degree to which the wife has separate control over economic resources. Movements to urban environments increase the opportunities for women to join the labour force, which would give women an independent income and thus a greater share in decision-making. However, we should be aware that authors such as Smock (1977) argue that women are in fact more subordinate in urban areas in places like Ghana because they often derive status from the husband's success rather than from their own activities.

With regard to polygyny, the relevant features include whether polygyny is a status symbol; if it is, then the husband increases his status and should have more power in the family. As the number of wives increases, the husband spends less time with each wife and each wife gains more power over her own children. The first wife had more power than any subsequent wife, and senior wives tended to have more power than junior wives.

As polygyny loses status in society, the husband's power will depend more on his ability to provide financial support and other care for his wives and children. When the wives are the ones providing support for themselves and their children, the husband is not as powerful in the family as when he is the major supporter.

3   The family and society

In this chapter we consider the family as it relates to urbanization, the economy, religion and law.

The family and urbanization
Urban environments and their impact on family change

Many of the so-called features of urbanization, such as the disintegration of the extended family, are characteristics of a particular cultural historical pattern of urbanization, the Western industrialized type of urbanization. Indeed, some urban theorists have recently argued that many of the social problems of urbanization are a result of the capitalist economic system of these cities rather than anything peculiar to the urban environment.

What we now consider are two universal urban features rather than cultural variations of urban environments – namely, density and heterogeneity of population. A high density of population implies in social terms that individuals have contacts with greater numbers of people than in rural settings. More contacts result in relationships becoming perhaps rather impersonal because individuals cannot develop intimate social relationships with too many people. If a family does not live close to other members of the extended family, high density of population could mean that they have little privacy from neighbours, who are also unable or unwilling to help solve problems or resolve conflicts.

A high density of population often means that there is great competition for housing in African cities so that families may not be living in conditions which satisfy their basic needs and preferences. African squatter areas are the clearest example of this. Families who live in such areas have tremendous problems with periodic fires, water shortages and infectious diseases. They know how difficult it is to raise a family in such places but have no alternative.

A high density of population also allows people who wish to deviate from the norms of good family living to do so quite easily because they are hidden in a largely anonymous environment. African sugar daddies or mommies are more common in urban areas than villages because their actions are easily concealed. Such daddies or mommies are married individuals who date young unmarried women or men and provide extra money, gifts and favours to these younger people. In other cases, men refuse to marry another wife in order to avoid wedding and bridewealth costs, and instead keep a woman in a flat at the opposite end of town from where they live with their families.

For our purposes, heterogeneity of population refers largely to mixtures between different ethnic and racial groups, unlike Western urban conceptions, which focus on class heterogeneity. Groups which have quite different marriage customs and cultural practices come into contact in towns. Although many individuals may live in cultural islands in the towns, increased contacts are likely to lead to some alteration in marital customs and more general cultural beliefs. This is especially the result when intermarriage between groups becomes more common. The opposite has also been observed – that is, the virtual elimination of intermarriage between groups in towns, although in rural areas intermarriage was quite common. It appears that this exclusion of intermarriage between groups is due to each group's need to maintain separate identities in the urban environment.

Demographic features

In African urban environments, there are certain demographic features of the population in general and of the family in particular which are critically related to the nature of the family. One of the important features is the sex ratio. A comparison of sex ratios in urban areas in East Africa in 1969 showed there were about 153 men for every 100 women in Kenyan towns; 146 men for 100 women in Ugandan towns; and 131 men for every 100 women in Tanzania. Normally the ratio of men to women should be about 100:100. Failing this, a variety of social problems arise. Many problems, both during the colonial period and in current times, are directly related to a major imbalance in the sex ratio. Such imbalances may lead to an increase in prostitution, temporary unions or high illegitimacy rates, all of which affect family stability.

In many of the countries like Lesotho, which supplies male migrant labour to South Africa, the sex ratio has been imbalanced for very long periods and has created numerous family problems. While women in the villages or in the towns of the labour-supplying countries live for many years without their husbands being present, the husbands may establish second homes in the places where they work and may eventually cut off ties with their home and family. The men tend to move into temporary sexual unions, and the traditional marriage customs may lose their meaningfulness in such urban settings.

Size of family has also been an important demographic feature distinguishing urban from rural African families. While in Ghana, for example, family size has decreased, in Upper Volta a decrease in urban family size was followed by a return to typical family size once incomes became sufficiently high and stable over a period of years. However, there are features of African urban areas which would suggest future decreases in family size. First, children's economic contributions to the family are less in urban areas. When children become more of a 'cost', parents may intentionally limit the size of their family. Second, for the middle and upper income groups, urban residence usually means a decrease in infant and child mortality because of improved medical facilities. (At first, families are larger because improved health coexists with the desire for large numbers of children.) Third, contraceptive knowledge and usage is greater in urban areas, which may lead to reduced family size in the next few decades after mortality patterns have stabilized at relatively low levels. Such knowledge may also simply widen the gap between children's births. The Upper Volta figures suggest that regardless of the number of factors which could lead to smaller families, families will remain large in African urban areas as long as there is a cultural value for a large number of children.

Finally, polygamy is likely to decrease in urban areas, though it will certainly not disappear for many years to come. Polygamy is more expensive in towns, especially because of the cost of housing and food. An extra wife in a rural area contributes to food production, though in the towns such a wife may not be able to contribute anything. It is also difficult to find suitable housing which permits wives the separation of living areas which exists in rural areas. With scarce resources wives may compete for assistance from the husband for their own children, with resentment and conflicts resulting from any inequalities. Clignet (1970) has made an extensive analysis of the differences in family structure in the Ivory Coast, and has shown how the urban environment may lead to more independence for wives if they are able to obtain wage employment.

Regardless of whether we are talking about family size or type of family structure, in terms of number of wives, it is clear that the urban African family is demographically approaching a family size of five to seven members, and is likely to remain much larger than Western urban families even after some adjustments for economic constraints on family size. As we shall see, larger families are quite advantageous in African urban areas in a number of ways, particularly in terms of employment and business enterprises. Variations in the demographic features are, of course, not only determined by the urban setting, but also by the socio-economic characteristics of the marriage partners.

The extended family and the urban environment

It was mistakenly assumed by early urban theorists that the urban environment inevitably destroyed the extended family, because of a type of environmental determinism. Let us first see how the urban environment could affect family relationships, and then consider the opposite situation where family could affect the nature of the urban environment.

One of the earliest studies of the family and the urban environment was Peter Marris's *The Family and Social Change in an African City* (1966), which dealt with the results of a relocation of families in an urban renewal project in Lagos. The book highlights the role of the urban environment in effecting changes in the family. When nuclear families were relocated away from their extended family members, the frequency of visiting decreased and mutual aid declined. Although the younger generation welcomed the freedom from the interference of the older generation in the new site, the older generation missed the former life style. Distance, then, was one of the major factors which altered family relationships by reducing opportunities for visiting and interaction.

Urban areas are also often more expensive to live in than rural areas. It is often financially impossible to feed and clothe a large extended family in town. One of the major sources of conflict is relatives coming to town expecting to live freely off working relatives. Such relatives may never find work but may cause serious financial problems in the family before they are finally told to leave.

On the other hand, the urban environment may have so many pressures that the extended family becomes stronger in response to such pressures, as argued by Oscar Lewis in his treatment of Mexican urban family life. In Africa, the extended family often financially assists migrants in towns, in order to help the migrant obtain work quickly. Younger relatives are often sent to towns to help care for children and housework while the mother works. Brothers may jointly purchase a plot in order to have some urban property where they can establish themselves in business. Those in urban areas are often given vegetables and chickens by relatives in rural areas.

Aldous (1962) reviewed a variety of studies on the cities of Brazzaville, Dakar, Lagos, Léopoldville and Stanleyville, and concluded that the extended family still functioned strongly in the urban environment in terms of the co-residence of two or more nuclear families, joint activities by the extended family, assistance exchanged among individual relatives and friendship networks of kin members. Although a similar comprehensive review for the last twenty years is not available, selected studies do confirm the continuance of the same pattern – that is, the extended family has become stronger in the urban areas in many ways. Even with numerous strains on the extended family, it would be very wrong to argue that the urban environment has significantly reduced the relevance of the extended family.

From the opposite perspective, African kin networks have influenced the nature of the urban environment so that it is not as isolating and destructive of the individual as in many Western countries. This has, in fact, been the common distinguishing feature of many of the western African towns of indigenous origin. In Yoruba towns, the customary residential unit was the lineage. People lived in close proximity to members of the lineage. This pattern determined much about the overall architectural arrangements of the town. One's position in a family also determined almost all other rights and duties in the towns, especially the right to hold political office. As Gugler and Flanagan (1978:131) indicate, the Yoruba corporate body based on family lineages holds and manages property, sees to the economic welfare of needy members, cares for children of parents who are incapacitated and arbitrates disputes among the members. The role of the lineage in organizing life in the urban environments continued until colonial pressures, particularly with reference to office-holding, weakened the control of the lineage.

In modern times, social networks in urban areas have made many African towns appear to be a composite of ethnic villages, Clyde Mitchell's well-known work on social networks, or personal linkages of individuals, first described the function of these networks in migrant adaptation in African towns. In fact, it is more accurate to say that Mitchell pointed out how migrants adapted while not really adapting!

The paradox lies in the fact that prior to Mitchell's work, migrants who lived and worked in towns were seen as having become either townsmen, totally assimilated to the urban environment, or tribesmen, totally attached to the rural environment. In reality, these 'townsmen' still maintained close ties with their home areas, in terms of their networks of friends, and had developed linkages with urban dwellers as well. Networks of friends in towns were often limited only to people from the home area, although this became less frequent over time. Migrants may not even learn the language spoken in town if they are able to obtain their needs through family members, a very few of whom may know the local language.

Housing design and family relationships

One of the erroneous views about African architecture is that before the colonialists arrived, houses were simple and of poor quality. Richard Hull (1976) points to numerous examples of high quality, elaborate structures in Africa in the pre-colonial period. It is reasonable to argue that this pre-colonial housing was better adapted to family needs and related well to local environmental problems and resources. Fathy's (1973) ability to keep family and kinship structures relatively intact, according to people's preferences, in an Egyptian relocation effort, is one of the most impressive attempts yet to integrate indigenous housing styles with advanced architectural knowledge. As a result of his planning, the families were able to stay near relatives if they so wished and to have a traditional style of house, which met family spatial and cultural needs very well.

Most of the housing intended for Africans in the colonial period was cramped and unfit for families. Colonial housing for Africans was predominantly a type of 'bed-space' housing where the architects planned only for the space required for a single worker, not for him and his family. Families were not expected to live in towns. When better housing was built in the last part of the colonial period, it was often directly copied from European styles, with few modifications made for local cultural needs or with little relevance for traditional family spatial needs.

Typical urban units for the lower and middle income groups usually have a kitchen area, a sitting room, two bedrooms and a bathroom. Parents usually occupy one bedroom, and children another bedroom. However, numerous problems arise. Relatives may come at any time and need to be provided with a sleeping place. Children are then sent to the sitting room, or use mats to sleep on the floor in order to accommodate the visitors. In some cultures specific relatives, like a mother, are not supposed to share toilet and bath facilities with her married son. In fact, traditional customs in the villages often required that sons have their own hut after they were a certain age, even if they were not yet married.

The presence in town of multiple wives is another dilemma. If a man is provided with one house with two bedrooms, it is obvious that there is a problem in accommodating two or more wives. For many cultural groups, wives were supposed to have separate houses, never living under the same roof. Furthermore, in the housing for the poorest in slums or squatter areas, the typical unit is one room. There is thus no privacy for parents, since parents and children share the same space for sleeping, eating and some leisure activities.

The family and the economy

In this section, the emphasis will be on how the family is both affected by and affects the economy. Here we use the term 'economy' in the broadest sense, as the total economic system of a country, from the local systems to the national and, where relevant, international level. We deal with the various modes of production, whether agricultural or industrial, and with various types of trading and business activities.

The effect on families of the economy

One of the major factors of the economy relevant to the family has been wage labour. Wage labour arose as part of the changes accompanying colonization. Workers were needed on the railways, in houses, on plantations and, at the end of the colonial period, in factories. Most of the wage labour in the colonial period was a direct result of colonial policies on land and taxation, which forced people to obtain wage employment. From the outset, the migration stream consisted almost exclusively of males.

In some countries, the females were actually forbidden to travel without written permission from their husbands during the colonial period. Culturally, female migration away from the family was discouraged, since women were thought of as keepers of the farm or homestead. Furthermore, men who worked in towns often returned to the village to select a wife since women in the town were thought of as being loose women and more likely to be infertile as a result of abortions or other problems supposedly related to their life style.

When men migrated to towns, many visited home frequently and often permanently returned to their families after their days as wage labourers were over. Women had to adjust to the male absence during migration by taking on the husband's duties or by relying on hired labour for more difficult tasks. In situations where migration involved a more permanent move from the village to the town, more men began forming new families in the towns, and some never returned home. Prostitution and other forms of sexual unions became more common. One example of such unions was the 'stranger-permit' marriage of Sierra Leone, which evolved from the practice of strangers paying an amount to the chief, thereby informing the chief of their intent to stay in a village. This enabled the stranger to be a possible marriage partner for any local woman. Many of these women were left alone after the husbands migrated out of the village for work. The permit later was given to women strangers, on payment. Once the woman had this permit her husband could not, when he rejoined her, get clan compensation for adultery, though he might still get bridewealth returned (Harrell-Bond and Rijsdorp, 1977).

In some places, male labour migration had positive effects: an increase in innovations and the adoption of labour-saving technology which permitted the wife more time for trading, even though she had lost her husband's labour (Hay, 1976). This is what happened among the Luos of Kenya during the 1930s, where women innovated in adopting improved hoe blades, farming of white maize and in using labour-saving techniques.

Colin Murray's *Families Divided* (1981), on the impact of migration on the family, looks at the problems of and adjustments made by families of Basotho workers employed in South Africa. Murray tells us that roughly 70 per cent of rural households are effectively managed by women (1981:155). The majority of these households have male heads who are absent migrants. Because of the unreliability of cash remittances from their husbands, these women face much insecurity in their lives. Their children run a higher risk of malnutrition and are more likely to be reared by more distant kin if the mother is also forced into wage labour.

It is also clear from Murray's book that labour migration makes the household units very unstable in terms of membership. Those actually living together vary drastically over time, as migrants leave and sometimes later return, as younger children are sent to and come back from other kin. What this means is that the family unit with members in long-term, day-to-day interaction with one another is very rare. Members may live apart for years, sometimes reuniting to live together for a short time before separating again. Certainly shared physical residence is not a common feature of Basotho families. The Basotho women who are left behind by husbands must often depend on sharecropping, which means the loss of half of one's crop. Women are forced to enter into sharecropping agreements because they often are without seed, oxen or enough land to raise a crop (Mueller, 1977). However, it would be mistaken to assume that since family members are physically separated, they are no longer part of the same family. Ritual obligations, ownership of property and distribution of earnings may all operate on the basis of an on-going relationship among absent and present members of a family. The likelihood of the household permanently disintegrating is, of course, very high. Yet one should also realize that if all the household members lived together the family might break up even more quickly since it is almost impossible to survive without the income from wage labour (Murray, 1981:102).

Finally, there are two arguments advanced by some who hold that labour migration may not be a major source of family disruptions, these arguments being briefly noted by Murray. Both arguments contain inherent biases. One argument is that if the African husband–wife relationship does (did) not require intimacy or strong emotional attachment, then separation because of migration is not a very severe hardship. Secondly, families of migrants have probably become so used to labour migration that they are not unduly disturbed by it – they are used to it! The obvious biases in these arguments include a lack of understanding of the nature of African marriage, wherein lack of open expression of affection is mistaken for lack of attachment, and the assumption that Africans should have a less satisfying life than other groups simply because they have managed to live with such adverse conditions for so long.

We should also note that wage labour often resulted in the formation of non-kinship groupings which began either to fulfil family functions or to force families to change their functioning. These groups include the more informal social networks, discussed under the section on the family and urbanization, and voluntary associations and labour unions. Wage labour, whether in urban or rural areas, often drew together people from many different ethnic groups. Once communication was eased by the adoption of a standard language for all workers or by the creation of a *lingua franca*, the formation of non-kinship groupings was rapid. Labour unions affected families in a number of ways: first replacing some economic functions of the family but also forcing families to change internal sex roles and authority patterns.

Ousmane's *God's Bits of Wood* (1962) is a novel based on the 1947–1948 strike of the railway workers on the Dakar–Niger railway line. When the workers' union went on strike, women in towns became major providers of food and water for their families. They often journeyed to distant villages, as the colonial authorities shut off town water supplies and made it almost impossible to get food in the towns. While children died of malnutrition, and men and women died during the fighting with police, family authority structures and the division of labour within the family changed very drastically. Women who were more secluded because of Islamic customs ventured to distant places without their husbands, protesting or carrying out subsistence activities. When men saw their wives defy colonial authorities or openly battle with police, they gained a new respect for them.

Caldwell (1977) pointed out that before independence all francophone governments maintained the practice of paying family allowances. Yet Ousmane indicates the struggle which took place before those allowances became a reality. Ousmane shows the colonial authorities using the 'African family structure' to their advantage to obtain unlimited cheap labour, but refusing to accept the same structure when it came to family allowances. In the case of family allowances the African family had too many wives and children from the authorities' viewpoint. Thus, although European railway workers were given family allowances, African workers were denied these allowances at first. Strikes were often aimed at eliminating such discrepancies, which made normal African family life impossible.

In addition to the impact of such factors as migration and union activity on the family, the introduction of a cash economy also had a great influence in altering family structure and functioning, even when migration did not occur. As Oppong notes, referring to Gough's work, the root cause of changes in kinship is

the incorporation of societies into a 'unitary market system'. Economically and jurally men and women become increasingly independent of kin groups, as access to resources and position of power depend more upon voluntary labour contracts and personal wealth, rather than rights in jointly held family estates (Oppong, 1981:7).

When, in the later part of the colonial period, cash crops were first grown by Africans, these crops tended to be owned by men in central and eastern Africa, although women usually provided the labour. The exceptions were in West Africa, where work from Polly Hill in southern Ghana shows that ownership of cocoa-farming land by women is common (Michelwait, 1976). In the 1970s it was still common for the sales from crops in East Africa to be marketed through cooperatives to which the husbands belonged. This meant that the husband did, and often still does, control the income from cash crops, even though his wife and children contribute much of the labour.

Cash crops usually result in the reduction of hectarage devoted to food crops. Because there are shortages of land and an increasing population pressure, cash crops are simply grown on land where food crops were formerly grown. The reduction in both the hectarage and the amount of time a woman was able to devote to her food crops led to a poorer diet and poorer health status of family members. Thus malnutrition often coexists with a sizeable income.

This problem partially results from the fact that because the husband controls the income, financial irresponsibility on his part would result in an inadequate diet for family members. As a woman's land area gradually declined, she was less able to provide enough food for her family. The woman lost her power over income and the fruits of her labour as the husband's control over those fruits of her labour increased.

Under the Programme for Better Family Living which is part of the family planning programme in most African countries, attempts are being made to help families manage such problems as malnutrition and child mortality. Parents are often introduced to improved agricultural techniques so that food production is better suited to family health needs. Mothers are given advice on health and nutrition so that they may know how to improve the family diet. Finally, family planning is expected to help reduce family health problems primarily through spacing of children. There is an underlying assumption that the family's level of living or access to resources must be improved as part of the whole process of educating people about the maintenance of family health.

In West Africa, for example, where women were the major traders, the cash crops were tended by the husbands. Thus, men did provide labour for these cash crops and often produced the food crops as well, since their wives were busy trading. In any case, West African men were the major producers of food crops long before cash crops were introduced, in families where the wife was the trader.

Changes in the family can also be traced to various projects which were intended to accelerate overall national economic growth and income. Projects included settlement schemes, dams and industrial centres. Settlement schemes shared a common feature: housing which was unsuitable for the large extended family or the polygamous family because the housing units were not large enough. The tenure system, in schemes where cash crops like rice were grown, forced families to disperse. Children of the tenants were not expected to settle permanently in the scheme, and even parents had no security of tenure, because this was tied to the ability to produce a specified amount of the cash crop. In other types of schemes where people were simply allocated land for which they had a title deed and the right to plant as they wished, women were seldom given title deeds. Through this type of land registration, women's rights over use of land decreased from what had been traditional.

Even today, men's ownership of the land means that women are further deprived in terms of economic opportunities. Loans are granted only to people with some security such as land. Here women still lose heavily compared to men. Women face barriers in terms of becoming large-scale farmers or businesswomen since they lack access to capital and land. Agricultural services tend to be biased towards men since they are the owners of the land, yet women are often the backbone of African farming systems.

Development projects such as dams and rice schemes have also adversely affected the family's health and hence total economic productivity. Diseases like schistosomiasis and malaria are often caused by the creation of artificial bodies of water which provide new breeding and transmission grounds for the disease vectors. There are also large parts of Africa, where diseases like leprosy and river blindness take disastrous tolls in human suffering and life, in places which may already have serious economic problems of underdevelopment. Such diseases limit the ability of individual families to participate fully in the economy, especially where there are no types of financial assistance available. Hence, the concern with elevating or maintaining the income of families as part of the process of economic development must include reference to the adverse consequences of development projects or the unintended 'neglect' of some families whose members are too ill to benefit.

Changes in the economic system from a subsistence to a cash economy, and the growth of commerce and industry have all led to the emergence of groupings of people which are based on their control of resources. These groupings, often called classes, are hard to identify in African settings for a number of reasons.

First, the actual amount of economic wealth and possessions may be hard to match with behavioural measures such as life style. There is, for instance, no evidence that the richest people are more likely to reduce interaction with kin-group members than the poorest people. In other words, although it is easy to divide people into income groups, it is much harder to determine which life styles are common to specific income groups on the African continent. After independence, most of the wealthier families gradually 'adopted' traditional African family life styles in terms of leisure patterns, visiting of relatives, preferred foods and emphasis on large families. During the colonial period the traditional life style and culture had been demeaned by the authorities, leading to the pressure on many African élite families to adopt the European life style with all its ramifications.

Second, the ethic of sharing of resources within the extended family unit reduces the amount of accumulation of wealth and partially limits the formation of rigid class groupings. The wealthier family members are still expected to assist the poorer members by paying for school fees, providing accommodation for relatives who are at school or seeking work, or by offering small loans for various emergencies.

Strains do exist. Some wealthier families are finding the responsibilities too great and are reluctant to honour all requests for assistance. However, the majority do feel tremendous pressure because they try to honour most requests even if it means sacrifice on their part. This sacrifice means that the extent of conspicuous consumption or display of wealth will occasionally be much less than would be the case without family responsibilities.

Classes are therefore hard to identify, and there are few studies which have provided details on class as it affects family life style and structure. However, research does reveal differences that exist between selected classes or socio-economic groupings in particular countries. Gamble (1963) in his study of the Temne family in Sierra Leone has perhaps the clearest delineation of families by class groupings. The chief or landowning families tend to have polygamous, arranged marriages and large families. Families of Muslim religious teachers are also polygamous and large (the average size being twenty-five to thirty persons). These Muslim families often have three generations in a household. There are also well-to-do families, which gained high positions as a result of jobs during the colonial period. Polygamy is practised by these well-to-do families, and men encourage their wives' involvement in trading by providing them with trading money.

Differences are more marked for other types of families. Skilled labourers tend to have smaller, monogamous families and share some duties with the wife. Unskilled workers' families are characterized by frequent domestic quarrels, and there is no sharing of duties between husband and wife.

Christine Oppong's book, *Middle Class African Marriage* (1981) reports on her survey of Ghanaian civil servants. Financial management of these families was segregated, in that husband and wife 'insulate most of their cash and property dealings from observation and control by their partners' (Oppong, 1981:91). There was more expectation by the wife in these middle-class families that the husband would help in some of the household duties, and indeed there were husbands who did willingly help their wives. Oppong's findings in the area of decision-making are discussed above (page 29). Overall, her work is the most promising in terms of future research on class and family in Africa, because the topics of decision-making, division of labour and financial management patterns are perhaps the most pertinent and easily measurable indicators of class influence in the family.

The family can be affected in numerous ways by the economy. However, we now shift emphasis to examine how the family could affect the economy. One could say that the family influences the economy primarily through its preparation of family members for roles in the national economy and by its selectivity in permitting some family members the option of being trained by society for various roles.

As part of the whole process of socialization, the family may so rigidly define sex roles that female children in particular may feel that being a wife and mother excludes most occupations in society. This situation has historically been true for many African families, and still continues in parts of the continent. However, new efforts are being made in African countries to alter parental conceptions of male and female capabilities. While writers like Marjorie Mbilinyi (1972) of Tanzania demonstrate that parents still favour sending boys as opposed to girls to and through school, as part of the United Nations Decade of Women (1975–1985) new efforts are being made to alter this situation. Chiefs sometimes participate in such efforts by convincing parents of the relevance of giving girls equal educational opportunities.

Increasing opportunities for family members to enter different trades or occupations partially relate to the family's facilitation or hindrance of members' access to non-formal education. Adult literacy classes are available, but men may refuse to allow their wives to attend. If they do allow wives to attend, the husbands may continue to discourage them by disparaging the practical usefulness of such training. Classes held at agricultural training institutes are more immediately useful, but women may be unable to attend because of family responsibilites. Any limitation the family puts on a member's access to such educational opportunities curtails the member's job opportunities. The family limits its members' opportunities either through direct prohibitions against entrance into certain activities or through indirect biases generated from the roles in the division of labour. A woman, for instance, may not necessarily be prohibited from attending farming classes but may feel too overburdened by her family responsibilities.

The family's acceptance of the role of women as traders or wage employees is another way in which the family affects the economy; that is, it determines the proportion of women involved in these sectors of the economy. In West Africa, it is more culturally acceptable for women to trade than it is in East Africa, with some ethnic groups having disproportionate numbers of women traders. However, even in West Africa, women are controlled by family duties with the result that most of them reduce trading activities when they have young children at home. This is true for both the Yoruba women (Marshall, 1964) and for Ibo women (Peil, 1975).

Women in East Africa do trade but have only recently engaged in long-distance trade, in which women of West Africa have long been involved. Kongstad and Monsted (1980:115–16) also note a strong relationship between the Kenyan wife's entrance into trading and the low level of economic support from the husband. They suggest that this relationship may be explained in two possible ways. It may be that the woman enters trading because the husband is a poor supporter, or that once she enters trading the husband reduces his support for the family. This does not mean that women are becoming economically successful, because most manage to stay only at a mere subsistence level. In this case, the family, through the husband, tends to limit the scale at which women can trade by altering responsibilities in response to the woman's trading income. This is in contrast to West Africa, where a woman is rewarded by her husband through his assistance in her ventures. For instance, among the Yoruba, the men provide trading capital for their wives after the marriage seems secure. A stable marriage thus enables women to enter into large-scale trading.

In some countries, the role of wife as wage earner results in family problems, whereas elsewhere it results in more happiness and satisfaction for all family members. De Lancey's (1981) study of women who work in a Cameroon tea estate showed that the wife's pay is usually greater than the husband's. The role of wife and wage earner are thus incompatible. On the other hand, in Nigeria, 36 to 50 per cent of the males interviewed felt that marriages were more stable when a woman worked because her position in the family was enhanced (Karanja, 1981). Karanja also noted that women were happier because they had more money to pay for obligations to their extended family group.

African women also became prominent entrepreneurs through intermarriage with Europeans who came during the colonial period. In Senegal, African women who married Europeans dominated commerce until the 1830s and 1840s. The women tended to be rich property owners (Brooks, 1976). It is not clear whether they received initial capital from their husbands or whether the fact of being married to a Portuguese man gave them special powers and privileges. Most likely they were both true to some extent, but the fact remains that it was through marriage that these women became very powerful.

More specific evidence on the link between African family systems and business enterprises is sparse, but it does seem from studies by Marris and Somersett (1971) that the African ethic of caring for relatives is an obstacle in the development of businesses. African families are often poor in resources and are bound by the norm of sharing wealth with relatives. When problems arise, the needs of the family members usually take precedence over the expansion of business.

Furthermore, business may compete with land in terms of investments of time and money. Unlike Asians, who identify family welfare with business, Africans tend to identify family welfare with the land. New parcels of land are more often purchased through profits from business than are businesses expanded with profits from agricultural produce, although the relationship does in fact operate in both directions. The fact is that land is preferred as a more stable form of security for the family than are business enterprises.

One final issue has to do with the sharing of resources among family members. This sharing can be both a cause and an effect relative to the economic system. Sharing, we have noted, can reduce input into productive enterprises like businesses. On the other hand, when the economy leaves one family wealthy and another poor, sharing can be a reaction to the harshness of the economic conditions. Adepoju (1977), in his study in Nigeria, found that in Ife, 62 per cent of those interviewed sent money home to the rural areas, and in Oshogo, 54 per cent sent money home. Work by Knowles and Anker (1981) shows that about 20 per cent of the salaries of low-income urban Kenyan workers is remitted to relatives in rural areas. This means that income figures by themselves are very misleading as indicators of the standard of living, the income being stretched over many families rather than one family.

Religion and the family

Treatment of the impact of religion on the African family has often been overly simplistic. Overt behaviour such as marriage ceremonies are used to prove that patterns of family life have changed drastically, while persistent underlying adherence to traditional African ethics and religious thought is often ignored by writers. To put it more simply, it has too often been assumed that the impact of religions like Islam and Christianity was very clear-cut and involved an almost total change of value systems. Recent evidence shows that in many cases there has been a merging of the traditional African values, a merging which is difficult to discern through overt behaviour patterns.

There is also a tendency by researchers to over-emphasize the impact of major world religions like Christianity and Islam to the exclusion of the numerous other smaller religious groups and sects. These smaller groups may indeed have a greater and more direct impact on family relationships than the major religions.

Before the intrusion of foreign religions, the traditional African religions had some common features which influenced the whole nature of family life. Of primary importance was the close relationship between the living family and kin members and the ancestors. This perhaps explains the elaborateness of ceremonies connected with every stage of the family life cycle, since ceremonies often enabled the living to maintain ties with non-living family and kin members. The idea of a person's life continuing, even after death, as long as the family remembered him or her, was common. It helps us understand why even when a man died, it was important for him to have children born in his name (as in the custom of levirate); these children would be thought of as his and would keep his memory alive. When misfortunes arose, people often atoned to the dead, assuming that the dead were angered by some behaviour of their living relatives. Maintenance of family shrines was believed to be crucial to the peaceful continuance of family life. Ancestors were believed to discipline family members if these members neglected familial duties or acted disrespectfully to older members.

African religions tended to pervade most of African life, unlike religions like Christianity which were often seen as having a very limited relationship to daily life (Mbiti, 1969:233). Pervasiveness can be seen in terms of explanations given for difficulty in childbirth, treatment of infertility, systems of respect among family and kin members, seclusion of mothers after birth, sexual abstinence rules and circumcision rites.

As Islam and Christianity spread throughout Africa, people did lose some of their traditional religious beliefs and practices, though many beliefs were retained and blended together with these religions. Although Mbiti (1969:220) argues that both Islam and Christianity are indigenous to Africa, we should realize that he is referring to very few parts of Africa, in particular Ethiopia and North Africa. Major penetration of Islam occurred from the eleventh to the twelfth century, when it spread over the North African region. Islam also spread throughout the East African coastal region. From the seventeenth to the eighteenth centuries there was a religious revival in the West African region, as some Muslim leaders in Islamic areas attempted to remove some of the African departures from Islamic codes of behaviour. Christianity began to have a major influence in the eighteenth and nineteenth centuries, when missionaries became widespread throughout the continent.

Islam had been seen by some scholars as more adaptable to African traditional beliefs than Christianity. Muslims were allowed to practice polygamy, and Muslims did not demand strict adherence to Islamic rites (Oded, 1974:234). Hence, many traditional customs were combined with the Islamic rites. Concubinage was an accepted practice, and both the concubines and their children had well-defined rights, obligations and status.

The spread of Islam meant the introduction of Islamic law, with its elaborate codes governing inheritance, family relationships and moral behaviour. It forbade levirate, and specified how marriage rites were to be conducted. One of these rites includes the inspection of the bed sheet used by the bride and groom on their wedding night, to see whether there was blood which would indicate that the bride was still a virgin. Punishments for infractions of moral codes, such as illicit sex, were very harsh at times. Although women were to be secluded from contact with male non-family members, Islamic law did allow women to inherit property. Eventually in Kenya and Uganda, for example, Islamic law was given statutory recognition, the law in Kenya being called the Mohammedan Marriage, Divorce and Succession Ordinance, and was originally enacted in 1920.

Islam also required the seclusion of women, in order to protect them from evil influences and from leading others into evil behaviour (primarily sexual deviations). The rule on seclusion was strictly observed, as in the case of the Hausa women from the ruling class who were completely secluded; and very loosely adhered to as in the case of the Baganda Muslims, whose women were and are seldom veiled or physically secluded. Yoruba Muslims do allow wives to go out to trade during the day (Cohen, 1969:60). Some women no longer help in farm work because of the seclusion rule, and others still work openly on their farms.

There are Muslim majorities today in Mali, Mauritania, Niger, Senegal, Somalia and Sudan, with a population of more than half a million. There are strong pluralities of Muslims in Guinea and Nigeria. Muslims have higher rates of divorce than other religious groups (Okediji and Okediji, 1966) and higher rates of child mortality (Sembajwe, 1981). The higher rates of mortality are probably due to less access to modern medical knowledge, reluctance to use medical services, or seclusion rules which make it difficult for women to attend public clinics.

Christianity spread through most of Africa during the colonial period. Missionaries were among the first Europeans to have rather intimate contact with the inhabitants, though the contact was often negative. With little knowledge of the values of the Africans, many of the early missionaries denounced the sacrifice to ancestors, magic, betrothal of children, inheritance of widows, polygamy, many types of songs and dances, initiation ceremonies and bridewealth. Such denunciations over time did undermine traditional customs and beliefs which had protected married life and kinship relationships. Certain Christian groups encouraged individualism, through such practices as urging parents to take more personal control over the moral upbringing of their children rather than relying heavily on the efforts of many relatives.

Most of the first schools on the continent were introduced by missionaries. Attendance at such schools sometimes involved a major break with family and traditional values. There were cases of individuals fleeing to missionaries to be protected from family members who would not accept conversion of family members to Christianity. Rifts among family members worsened in places where Christians received special privileges, such as Kenya, where in the 1930s some Christians were exempted from forced labour. In other cases, attendance at schools led some to despise their parents' illiteracy and way of life.

In all fairness to the churches, we should realize that they did encourage the education of women as much as that of men. Women were thus afforded new opportunities for mobility, which often directly affected their power within the family.

It has been suggested by Kisembo and his co-authors (1977:6) that many Africans who are nominally Christians refuse to marry in church because of the fear of the indissoluble and monogamous nature of Christian marriage. Actually, the churches vary in their handling of divorce, the Roman Catholics being the most rigid, totally forbidding divorce and allowing only limited grounds for nullifying a marriage. Some Anglican communities on the continent do allow divorced individuals to remarry in church, and they may even be readmitted to communion in some dioceses. The Anglicans also attempted in the 1920s and the 1930s to Christianize African religious beliefs and practices among the Masai in Tanzania. One example is male initiation ceremonies which were altered in include the names of saints instead of the names of the great ones of tribal past. At the end of seclusion each boy makes a confession, and no new name is given after the ceremony as was traditionally done (Ranger, 1972).

No attempts were made by the European Christian groups to accommodate female circumcision. In fact, the practice was very strongly opposed. Most opposition centred solely around the physical operation, which was most often clitorectomy. Christian responses revealed almost total ignorance of the wider significance of the practice. Female circumcision involved a great deal of preparation of the female children for their adult roles. This preparation included provision of knowledge about personal hygiene of the woman, sexual matters, treatment of one's husband, care of children, moral behaviour and various duties of a woman in the society. More importantly, the girls formally became women. They learned to bear pain and to discipline themselves, and were recognised by all members of the community as women worthy of respect and acceptable for marriage. In some groups, it was an abuse to tell someone that he or she was the child of an uncircumcised woman. Circumcised women also seemed more able to stand up to men to defend their cultural rights. However, circumcision did not mean that women became staunch opponents of men or competitors for household power and authority. Rather, women became confident in performing their roles in society and in knowing how to limit male mistreatment of them as wives while still submitting to the husband's rightful authority in most matters.

Even today, opposition to the practice from groups outside Africa refers to the practice as a type of physical abuse. Again, this view is so narrow that there seems to be little basis for discussion between supporters and opponents of the practice. Currently, some governments have banned the practice, yet circumcision still continues in secrecy, though with less frequency. The practice has begun to lose some of its practical significance since many groups have been forced to drastically shorten the time period from several months to a matter of days. Thus, the wider educational value decreases with the shortened time period and lack of open support. In other places, there may be various types of revivals of the practice. In Zambia, one indigenous African church has re-introduced female circumcision, it now being a formal ceremony within the religious services (Jules-Rosette, 1980).

Finally, Christian Churches have tended to oppose the widespread, indiscriminate distribution of birth control methods. Recently, the Presbyterian leaders in Kenya urged that unmarried persons be refused birth-control devices. The Roman Catholic Church has strictly forbidden all artificial methods of birth control including the pill and sterilization. Since traditional periods of total sexual abstinence are disappearing, there is a need for couples to have some control over their fertility. Many couples using artificial birth-control methods are likely to continue participating normally in Church services without feeling greatly inhibited by Church proclamations. In other words, their refusal to accept rules on birth control is not seen by them as a major infraction which should lead them to be excommunicated from their Church.

The Roman Catholic African bishops' contribution to the 1981 Synod on the Family in Rome sought to clarify the relationship between the Church and the African family. First, it was stated that marriage was seen to be both personal and communitarian since the two individuals marrying had an immense responsibility in bringing forth life, which ensured the security of their respective lineages. Second, marriage was considered a process, with successive stages rather than one ceremony as in Church doctrine. Dowry was seen as having too many disadvantages at the present time – among them that it has become too difficult for young men to raise the amount required, and that it often makes the husband believe that he owns his wife.

African bishops at the Synod also noted that currently the practice has become common of people marrying first according to tribal customs and then later having a church wedding. Since very often the first marriage ceremony is crucial to the couple's acceptance within the kin group and large tribal community, the second ceremony is often thought of as an extra though not an essential ceremony for the validity of the marriage. Furthermore, it was seen as wrong to refer to tribal marriages as 'trial marriages' since they in fact are not at all trials and are strongly supported by the community. The bishops therefore requested that more attention be given to what is actually happening in Africa today rather than giving sole consideration to basic Church principles. Hence, a practice like polygamy should be treated cautiously. When polygamous families are already long established and conversion takes place, these people should be approached with patience, rather than pressured into unrealistic courses of action with regard to their family members. Much of the issue of the relationship between Church and the family revolves around the respect for diverse cultural forms of the family.

Although the major religions like Christianity and Islam have had their impact, the African independent churches and smaller sects should not be ignored. The formation of many of the independent churches was precipitated by the almost wholesale rejection of African culture and customs by the Christian churches. The majority of the customs were directly related to marriage and family matters. Polygamy, for instance, is accepted in most independent churches, as are many other customs like circumcision which were rejected by some churches.

The smaller sects also attempted to incorporate more of African culture into the religious belief systems, though the incorporation was perhaps less systematic. More emphasis was given to conversion as a major process rather than to rigorous formulation of doctrine. In some respects, the sects model the traditional cults, which were usually segregated in terms of sex.

Writers like Robins (1979) argue convincingly that women were able to escape traditional family role constraints through membership in such groups. Accounts of the conversion of women leaders of these groups suggest that many were unwilling or unable to fulfil normal wifely or motherly roles, and thus managed a change in their roles through the adoption of an important religious role.

Related to sects are cults of spirit possession which have more in common with traditional systems of belief and are seldom offshoots of any Islamic group or Christian church, though they may co-exist with either religion. Hoek-Smith and Spring (1978) argue that in both Islamic and Christian communities in Africa spirit possession has often enabled women to compensate for a lack of authority and lack of freedom in family and kin group affairs. Among the Yoruba, similarly, witchcraft, as with spirit possession, permitted women great power. Men also joined cults headed by old women if they were having reproductive problems (Hoek-Smith and Spring, 1978: 250, 265).

Some authors see spirit possession as a way of relieving tension due to the migration of husbands (Sibisi, 1977). However, Wilson (1977) argues that competition among co-wives or women in general causes an increase in spirit possession rather than competition between males and females.

The family and the law

Legal systems in Africa are both a rich source of detail about family conflict and an actual cause of much family change and conflict. The basic obstacles include the fact that in most nations of Africa there is seldom one predominant national culture or life style that would justify having one family legal system. This situation has resulted largely because of the historical origin of African family law. The close relationship between African family law and family conflict and change derives from the whole process of development of the national legal systems.

During the colonial period, statutes of the colonial powers were introduced into the colonies while at the same time the numerous customary legal systems were allowed to continue. When there is no unitary system of family law in a country there is more likelihood of conflict, since many people may not know which laws apply to them or their general legal rights under the laws. Even the courts may have difficulty deciding which laws apply when each party to a marriage comes from a different ethnic group or cultural community. Even with a unitary system there would still be problems until most ethnic groups truly accepted the national family legal system.

Development of African family law

From the beginning of the colonial period, most African countries experienced three phases in the development of family law. First, there was a period when the British, French and other foreign statutes were applied to settlers in the colonized territories. Settlers were thus capable of continuing their style of life with the same legal system that they would have had in their home country. Each distinctive community was to be subject to its own family legal system. Even at the present time, this phenomenon of multiple systems of family law continues to pose problems to legislators and the ordinary man. A common situation is that in which an African nation has many customary laws and an Islamic and a Christian or civil variety of family law. Kenya, in fact, has all of these varieties as well as a Hindu marriage law.

In the second phase, there were attempts by the colonial powers to extend the applicability of the foreign laws to the indigenous people who had adopted many of the customs and behaviour of the foreigners (or settlers). Judges were confronted with two pressing problems: intermarriage between people of two ethnic or cultural groups, and changes in the nature of the marriage. Where there was intermarriage, the issue was 'conflict of laws', meaning that two very different sets of laws could validly be applied to settle a case. However, the judge would apply only one type of law if the two laws were in conflict with one another.

For individuals who were from the same community, changes in the nature of the marriage occurred in two ways. Some couples re-married under a different type of family law than the one which they had originally been married under. Judges then had to determine the nature of the marriage on the basis of the couple's perception about its nature and upon what the intention of the couple was in marrying under a second system. Most other cases of changes in the nature of the marriage resulted from changes in life style, such as the adoption of monogamy after having at first married under customary law (which is potentially polygamous). To give one example, we look at the Lesotho law briefly.

The factors which are regarded by the judiciary as indicators that a Masotho (from Lesotho) has adopted a European way of life and should have marriage cases heard under common or civil law rather than customary law are:

1) living in towns
2) no ploughing or grazing rights in rural areas
3) employment in professions, business – civil jobs
4) owning a car
5) wearing of European clothes
6) having a savings account
7) ownership of life insurance policies
8) adherence to Christian faith
9) civil marriage
10) education of children in government or mission schools
11) eating meals together (husband and wife) (Poulter, 1977).

Even then, Poulter notes that such indicators may not be very practical since Basotho live in two worlds, African and European. It would be unfair to apply either form of law rigidly to such people.

During the second phase, another major feature was the increasing predominance of the law of the colonial power over indigenous customary laws. The colonialists, as part of their 'civilizing mission', felt it was their duty to alter indigenous customs and beliefs until they conformed with the laws of the colonial power. This was based on the assumption that the colonial law was a superior one, and one of the major proofs put forward was the fact that the laws were derived from the so-called 'natural rights' of man.

In British colonies, the phrase 'repugnant to justice and morality' illustrates why the assumption of superiority over indigenous laws was both unrealistic and biased. The phrase meant that customary laws were to be applied to the respective community members only if the laws were not 'repugnant to justice and morality'. Whose justice and morality? British justice and morality. In actuality, the phrase was used to discourage customs which were unacceptable to British culture. It was thus a question of whose cultural values would predominate rather than whose values or behaviour were more just or moral.

To elaborate on this point, we look at the concept of marriage itself. According to *Hyde v. Hyde* (1866), a marriage is a voluntary union for life between two individuals to the exclusion of all others (the words 'for life' have been ignored since divorce became increasingly common from the mid-twentieth century). Thus, monogamous, not polygamous, marriages were treated as true marriages in this second phase. For instance, although persons married by civil law could not give evidence in courts against each other, those who were married polygamously did not meet the criteria for 'marriage' according to *Hyde* v. *Hyde* and thus could give evidence against each other.

Secondly, the emphasis on the statutes of colonial powers as opposed to indigenous customary law was also related to the fact that indigenous customary law was unwritten. Only, in fact, in the 1970s with the Restatement of African Law project was a comprehensive effort made by many countries, including Botswana and Kenya, to compile details of customary laws. Within each country this often meant compiling details on laws for many different tribes. For example, in Botswana's Restatement of African Law volume entitled *Tswana Family Law* (Roberts, 1972) there are laws given for eight tribes. Each country involved in the project has a separate volume on family law.

The only problem is that perhaps this summary of customary laws has come too late since the third phase is characterized by national attempts to develop one system of family law that could apply to all people in the country, regardless of their tribal or ethnic group. Most often this one system of family law is largely the family legal system of the former colonial power. Kenya's 1974 Law of Succession epitomizes the problem. This law is intended to provide rules on succession or inheritance that would be generally applicable to all the people of Kenya. It is largely modelled on British notions of inheritance, and seems based on the hidden assumption that the customary laws of inheritance could not adequately deal with modern forms of property like cars and businesses (Kuria, 1977). Furthermore, this law of succession exists in a situation where there still are four separate laws on marriage, covering its celebration, validity, dissolution and so on. Tanzania also attempted to consolidate its marriage laws.

Contrasts among laws

We now turn to a selective review of central aspects of family law, contrasting typical customary laws and modern civil law. Although the specific details differ from country to country, there are many features of the law which hold true for most African countries.

Capacity to marry

The customary criteria for an individual's capacity to marry often include the following. The persons to be married should 1) have reached puberty; 2) have gone through some type of preparation for marriage, often a circumcision ceremony; 3) be free of diseases like leprosy; and 4) be mentally sound or sane.

For a civil marriage, capacity includes the following: 1) an age requirement, usually the age at which one becomes an adult legally according to national laws; 2) single status of both parties; 3) both parties should not be from prohibited degrees (for instance, first cousins are prohibited from marrying each other according to most civil laws in Africa and most parts of Europe, and in South Africa, people from different races are not allowed or do not have the 'capacity' to intermarry with other racial groupings); 4) parental consent is needed only if those to be married are under the age of legal adulthood; and 5) freedom from diseases such as syphilis, or serious mental illness.

Validity of the marriage

Under most customary laws a marriage is valid if 1) bridewealth has been paid; 2) required ceremonies of marriage were performed; and 3) the parties had the capacity to marry.

For a marriage to be valid under civil law, 1) the marriage ceremony has to be performed by a authorized person to perform it; 2) the ceremony has to be performed in a place of worship or in a building which is legally registered for such an activity; 3) there should be witnesses to the ceremony; and 4) the parties to the marriage must have the capacity to marry.

Inheritance of property

In most patrilineal customary systems the wife does not inherit land or property, although she is normally granted usage rights over pieces of land which she farms. Women's rights included, for instance, among the Luo of Kenya, 'access to communal grazing lands, farmlands, water supply and hills where firewood could be collected, as well as access to fish, and naturally growing fruits, vegetables and herbs' (Okeyo, 1980;195).

Indeed, no individual inherits property in the sense that the true heir is the family. Men, in a patrilineal society, represent the family, and land is passed down from father to son. Men make decisions about the allocation of the land, and in many groups it is only after marriage that a son may be able to participate in such decision-making.

Okeyo (1980:199) indicates how colonial policies altered the land rights of women. As a result of colonial intervention such as direct legislation and general labour policies, pressure was put upon customary tenure institutions. One of the results was that 'family heads assumed greater autonomy in decisions regarding cultivated land' (Okeyo, 1980:200). Women still have some usage rights, but Okeyo argues that these rights are much less permanent than was traditionally the case. This is so because men have become the individual title owners under land reform programmes, and thus are able to alienate the land without consulting the larger family or communal group. This situation is paralleled in many other African nations where land was registered to individuals in the latter part of the colonial period.

Coker's *Family Property among the Yorubas* (1958) and Obi's *Modern Family Law in Southern Nigeria* (1966) both deal with the problems connected with the alienation of land in Nigeria. Coker's is perhaps one of the more complete treatments of the specific functions of the extended family relative to various types of property and rights over property.

In African countries where land alienation did not occur, land still belongs to the family. For matrilineal groups this land is inherited through females, whereas, as noted above, in patrilineal groups, the line of inheritance is the male one. Rules about other forms of property are much more diversified. However, property brought to the marital home belongs to both husband and wife among the Hausa.

Among nomadic groups, rights to cattle and grazing areas replaces rights to arable land. Upon marrying, women are often given a certain number of cattle or other animals over which they have rights of use in the sense of obtaining milk but seldom the right to sell or otherwise dispose of the animals.

Modern civil laws of inheritance emphasize the right of individuals to write wills, whereby they leave their property to persons of their choice rather than to their family. When a person has died having left a will, he is said to have died testate, while one who has not left a will has died intestate.

Children can inherit from parents regardless of their sex in most modern systems. What affects their right to inherit is their legitimacy, with the legitimate children usually having more rights than illegitimate children in cases where the parent has died intestate. There have been efforts in some African nations to alter this situation so that illegitimacy does not affect the inheritance rights of children.

Islamic laws of inheritance are still in force in the majority of African countries where there are substantial numbers of Muslims, although there may be only specific parts of a country where Islamic laws take precedence over customary or civil law. Under both Islamic law and customary law, illegitimate children had almost the same rights as legitimate children. In the Islamic system, children were distinguished from one another in terms of whether their mother was wife or a concubine (Stroebel, 1979). Customary laws did not really have a notion of illegitimacy in the sense that a child was born into his father's (in a patrilineal society) or his mother's (in a matrilineal society) kin group.

Custody of children

At various times the question may arise as to who should have the right of custody over children. Most often this question occurs in cases where the parents are separated or divorced or where both parents are dead. There are fewer examples of custody decisions involving parents who are still living together but are accused of neglect or physical or mental abuse of the child. In these examples, which are rare in Africa, the children could be given to other relatives or taken over by children's homes or institutions.

According to customary law, the children were actually in the custody of an extended family unit, so that illness or death of parents simply entailed a relative taking over responsibility for the child. However, in modern civil law, the biological parents or legally acknowledged parents of the child have the first right to custody. Conflict over custody in recent years in Africa has been largely centred on the issue of custody of children born to married women from irregular unions. Traditionally, the children would have gone to the husband because he had paid bridewealth (in patrilineal systems). In the last two or three decades, courts have been increasingly inclined to grant custody to the woman of children who were fathered by a man other than her husband, if the marriage does break down.

Dissolution of marriage

Marriages can be nullified or a divorce granted for various reasons. Marriages are typically nullified if either party did not have the capacity to marry or if one party knowingly concealed an infertility problem from the other. Grounds for divorce include adultery, desertion, cruelty, being of an unsound mind or being found guilty of rape, sodomy or bestiality.

4 Conflict and the family

The fact that Africa has been going through many social changes has been documented in detail by many writers. These changes have not spared the African family. It is now well established that the African extended family systems have been experiencing major changes, and forms of nuclear family systems can now be found in Africa, especially in the urban areas. This process of change has exposed the African family to varied problems, some of which have been discussed earlier. These changes, especially those concerning the extended family system, have generated considerable conflicts of prescribed norms and behaviour among families in Africa. These conflicts are centred on marriage; roles; African life style; land tenure and inheritance; certain forms of diseases like mental illness, leprosy and epilepsy; leisure-time needs; rural–urban migration; and working mothers (to mention only a few).

Problems related to marriage in general

In Africa, because mate selection depended very much on the parents, choosing a spouse was very much a family affair. Both families scrutinized each other before an association was made. This scrutiny was important because it took care of differences in values, expectations and life styles. Therefore, those considered witches ended up marrying witches, and this similarity of background facilitated the adjustment of spouses although they might have been total strangers to each other.

The family not only participated in mate selection, but it also paid and received the bridewealth in situations where the practice existed. Both families took each other very seriously, and entered the contract fully aware of what was expected of each party. This particular involvement was useful when problems cropped up in marriage as the same group pooled resources to remedy the problem. It also follows that the marriage was celebrated on very clear terms observing certain rituals which did not need to be expensive. In general, payment of bridewealth was never completed, and this to some extent rejuvenated the marriage as there was always something interesting to look forward to. For example, when the wife realized that her husband no longer paid attention to her, she could always remind her husband, 'You have not yet finished with my parents'. The husband, realizing this obligation, might attempt to be nice to the wife so that he was not harassed about the payment.

Adjustment to marriage seemed to have been made easier through the preparatory process that took place before it. In Africa for the most part individuals who felt ready to get married were taught how to behave towards their spouses. For example, among some tribes girls and boys were actually taught how to be romantic to each other. Besides, there were willing relatives to assist with information regarding marital relationships whenever needed. For the most part, the bride and the bridegroom were supported by the relatives throughout their adjustment period, and issues related to sex and other habits freely and confidentially discussed.

In situations where a woman could not bear children to her husband, arrangements to have other wives were amicably made. For example, when a woman was barren a second or a third wife was brought into marriage with her full consent. Besides, in some tribes in Africa she was even allowed to marry a wife who could bear children on her behalf. She could also choose the man the woman could bear children with. In few cases did the man make an independent decision to bring another wife without consulting his elder wife.

For the most part, relationships were well defined for the couples and they knew exactly how to relate to their relatives. For example, the way in which the couples related to their parents was not the same as the way in which they related to their brothers and sisters. In certain situations distances were kept through well-calculated taboos, whereas in other situations joking relationships existed. All this prevented situations which might have led to incestuous relationships and other forms of conflict that families experience today.

Now let us examine what has been happening recently and what is happening in marriage since Africa began to become 'enlightened'. For the most part the selection of a mate has now become an individual affair with less parental participation. The individuals intending to get married usually inform their parents about the decisions they have made. Some parents accept these decisions, whereas others denounce them. In situations where they are denounced the parties proceed with their plans and get married. Some of these decisions are hastily made, either because the girl became pregnant or the parties have fallen in love and so wish to marry as soon as possible. Not all marriages fit this category, and at times parents force their daughters and sons into marriage for fear of pregnancies or when daughters have become pregnant and those involved are not willing to accept marriage. At times different parties decide to try out marriage by living together with no formalities. Whatever method used, the parties intending to get married are often ill-equipped for marriage, and sometimes what they know is based on what they have read in books which at times portray an ideal picture of marriage, often in its Western form. The parties often learn with regret that the ideas presented in books actually do not exist in marriage for the most part. This in turn causes many frustrations for newly married couples.

Since the parents might have not participated in the decision regarding mate selection, they at times refuse to help with the payment of the bridewealth. Hence, in some situations the boy, with the help of the girl, pays the bridewealth, a situation that throws on to the young couple many financial burdens. Modern marriage in Africa is dominated by high expenditure, and families throw huge parties for their relatives and friends, often at the expense of the newly married individuals. The marriage celebration that should be humble and mainly to fulfil certain rituals has become a competition among families for the latter to expose their wealth. Because of the competition, those intending to get married at times actually acquire heavy debts, mainly in order to put on a good show, and newly-weds often start their married lives under financial strain. This creates many conflicts in marriage and makes adjustment difficult.

Although some aspects of the family have been changing and individuals can now choose the partners they like, Africa still remains traditional in some aspects. For example, the hospitality and the generosity of the African life still exist. Relatives and friends are allowed to come into the house whenever they want, and families are obliged to look after their relatives without any question. Here we have to consider those families living in rural areas and those living in urban centres.

In rural areas, because of the availability of space and the prevailing subsistence economy, life is still easy and the families can still entertain other relatives living with them with little strain. Here the relatives are indeed useful, as they provide free labour and their time is in fact well occupied. Newly married couples often enjoy privacy, as they may have a small hut to themselves; relatives staying with the family might actually be occupying another hut used as a kitchen or as a guest house. Hence the frictions that often accompany such hospitality tend to be under control in these circumstances. However, the rural family faces a problem when the young wife is left in the rural community because her husband has to go and work or look for employment in the town.

Sometimes she is left with young children to look after under the overall care of her in-laws. The separation generates a lot of problems not only because she has to look after the children single-handed as well as attending to the family's farm (garden), but she also tends to have numerous demands made on her by the in-laws. Being in the same vicinity, she is supposed to feed the entire family – that is, the in-laws and other relatives as well as her children. She is expected to work for her mother-in-law to prove whether she is really a good woman or not. (A good woman is one who fetches water and firewood and cooks for her mother-in-law.) She is also supposed to be sent everywhere like a child. Hence her major role to the in-laws becomes that of a servant to the family. The married daughters of the home come back to supervise. For example, they are concerned whether she is looking after the husband's parents and how she receives them when they visit. Usually they are unconcerned with her work load in the family.

If she fails to perform well, major friction arises between the woman and her in-laws. Letters may be written to the absent husband about her bad behaviour, leading to a poor relationship between the wife and the husband as well. Sometimes the husband takes sides with his family (parents, siblings and other relatives). The woman, feeling unsupported, may run away, and the marriage is dissolved, to the disadvantage of the children. Where the parents expect help from their son, often they demand part or all the money that he sends to their daughter-in-law, and if she refuses to give it to them she is blamed for monopolizing the son. In fact, if the son fails to send them money or sends less than they expect because he is attending to his family's needs first, the wife is not only likely to be blamed but also thoroughly condemned for having spoilt their son, and it will be claimed that she is siphoning off all her husband's money to her own family. She is often maliciously accused of selfishness or lack of respect, and otherwise verbally abused. The husband is expected to help his parents, sisters and brothers, their children and any other relatives within the extended family system. For the most part the help should be given to the members of the extended family before he thinks of his wife and children. All this creates problems for the family, as the family income is often expected to be shared among the members of the extended family and, considering the general salaries in Africa, the income is often over-stretched.

In towns adjustment is rather difficult. For the most part, space is often limited, and one has not only to buy all the services that are needed but also living space, food and every commodity. The ability to buy depends on earnings. Because employment is a problem in African towns and because the majority of the people in Africa are not well educated, it means that a large group of Africans move into towns looking for jobs which do not exist or for which they are not qualified. Thus, the majority of Africans living in towns are actually poor. Nevertheless, African hospitality and generosity is still with us, so most Africans looking for jobs in the towns have to, and expect to, stay with relatives – who are considered fortunate to work in towns, where most services and other forms of amenity are concentrated. Many Africans virtually live with relatives, either seeking jobs or getting education. Hence one enters marriage with a fleet of relatives, living with a spouse depending on whether accommodation is available.

In fact, because the situation is rather desperate, the African for the most part seems not to bother about privacy. There is a great willingness to share a room and even a bed. Relatives will agree to spend nights on chairs, in corridors or kitchens or wherever space may be available. Some relatives may not spend the nights in the house but come only for meals. Because large areas of Africa are rural, some relatives come to towns for curiosity; others come to stay either because they have been transferred or they are in transit to other rural communities and, because of the distance, must stay with relatives. Most Africans would regard staying in hotels as alien, and anyway they are sometimes too expensive. Usually, travellers are accompanied by their families, which may be quite large, including, for example, several children, a maid, a wife and a husband. Whatever the purpose of the visit, relatives expect to be looked after by the host – a task which is at times demanding. They expect to be made to feel at home. This means buying special food, providing clothing, bedding, soap and anything else the visitors may need.

Perhaps it is safe to say that the concept of separateness seems not to exist among African visiting relatives. At times they monopolize the activities in the household, and a stranger may find it difficult to differentiate the visitor from the owner of the house. These relatives seem not to bother about expenses, and they freely use water, food, electricity and anything else in the house as if these commodities come from an everlasting fountain. They may demand to be taken to visit other relatives and they expect the host to pay for transport. The partial education that most Africans receive tends not only to prepare them inadequately, but also instils in them unfounded self-confidence. This means that they may stay as visitors for a very long time rejecting any employment that may be available as they consider themselves suitable for superior jobs. The false self-perception may even lead the visitors, especially the men, to shun certain duties in the house and common foods and prefer to stay idle the whole day waiting for the delivery of special food. Failure to get this may lead to hostility towards the host. This is often shown through comments made about the spouse, length of stay in the bathrooms if there is one, utilization of available resources in the house and untold gossip about the family.

The behaviour described above tends at times to affect the family severely, especially the married couple. An African newly married couple may enter marriage not only with lack of privacy, but with endless burdens put on them. Budgeting becomes impossible, and saving for most couples becomes a white man's luxury. The life style becomes a hand to mouth one, and the African then lives for that particular moment. The burden is aggravated by the fact that part of the couple's income has to be remitted to the couple's parents living in the rural area. Therefore, the priority for newly married individuals becomes not how they should understand themselves as a couple, but how to look after the relatives and manage other problems in the extended family.

This focus on the problems of others rather than those of the couple may, however, actually lead to more stable marriages. For example, where personal problems might have been too painful and if unresolved might have led to the breakdown of marriage, in this situation the painful problem is no longer faced in the preoccupation with other people's problems. None the less, the trend is not useful, especially to children, and for the most part it leads to the empty marriages which seem to be common among Africans. It may also lead to situations where people run away from the burden through abuse of alcohol, spending time and nights away from home, which is quite common among African urban men. It can also lead to depression which is common among African women. Where spouses have heeded the complaints about their partners, marriages have actually been broken, and wives have left their husbands blaming the husbands' relatives for breaking up their marriages.

One of the things that has not changed much in the African family is the value placed on children. Children are still seen as the security system of most Africans in old age. It is even better if among the children there are sons. In fact, the status of an African woman improves if she has children, and this becomes yet more elevated if she has sons. This means that in situations where a couple fails to have any children for various reasons, many problems are faced. For example, when a man has realized that he could not have children in traditional society, he accepts his limitation, and arrangements were made secretly with his full consent for his wife to have children either with a close relative or a friend whom he trusted would not let him down by either divulging the arrangement or taking the wife from him. If the wife is the one with the fertility problem, arrangements are made for the husband to marry another wife or for her to marry her own woman, as described above.

The problems faced by couples who cannot have children nowadays are many. For the most part men tend to blame women for infertility even before consulting modern physicians. Often men marry other wives without consultation with the first wives. Hence relationships often suffer, leading at times to suicide attempts or dissolution of marriages. Although medical facilities are now available and can sometimes enable the couples with fertility problems to have children, these facilities are not used effectively, and squabbles still continue in the families faced with a fertility problem. In situations where a woman is only able to give birth to daughters, for the most part her husband becomes rather uncooperative, and may not only show resentment to the wife, but also to the daughters, and he may not even support them. He often acquires other wives in the hope of getting sons. Although this may create hostility within the family, leading to untold problems, it may also lead to unnecessarily large families. The wife, realizing that she can gain high status in the community only by having sons, may decide to continue bearing children until she gets a son. This situation has led to incidents where a woman produces seven to ten children before she has a son. This may in part explain the unnecessarily high birth rate in Africa.

Specific problem areas of families
Urban–rural migration

The urbanization process in Africa has been rapid, and there has been much movement of people from rural areas to urban centres, mainly to look for jobs and to enjoy the facilities that are usually concentrated in these centres.

Rarely does the African move with his family into town. For the most part, the family often remains in the country to look after the family property, mainly the land, while the head of the family looks for a town job. Once the job is acquired, the man remits part of his income to the family in his rural home. Thus, generally, most Africans living in the towns actually have two homes – a country and a town home. This arrangement creates conflicts for the family in general.

The first problem the family encounters with the above arrangement is the separation of the family where one gets the father staying alone in a town (at least, for some time) and the mother and the children living in the rural area. Because of the loneliness that is at times characteristic of life in towns, the father may get involved in other forms of relations, leading, perhaps, to infidelity or lack of commitment to any form of relationship. For example, it is common to find a man in the town having a woman friend and bringing up children with her which he may not consider really to be his children. Eventually, when he ends his job, he may disappear from such a relationship as if he had not fathered any child. While involved in other forms of relationship, he may neglect his rural family, a situation that leads some women to abandon their rual homes and come to stay with their husbands in the town. If this happens, the rural home may not only remain undeveloped, but the family may be constantly subject to quarrels between the spouses on how the sparse resources should be spent. The woman may develop suspicions about the husband's involvement in other relationships in her absence.

The possession of two homes tends to limit the family's ability to develop either of them. Although the man may be committed to develop his rural home, he may not have the resources to do so. Having lived in a town for some time and perhaps adopted town life, he may be ambivalent as to where he would like to settle when he retires. The fact remains, however, that most Africans end up hoping that when they retire they will develop their rural homes. Their town homes are not considered seriously, as life there is often thought to be transient. This unfortunate but unavoidable arrangement may be responsible for high death rates among retired African males, which tends to be premature. It seems that the best years of the African life span are spent undecided about what to do about the homes, and often when the decision is finally reached, it becomes impossible to develop a rural home in the late years of life. This may explain to a certain extent the underdevelopment of the rural community.

Having a father in the town and a mother and children at the rural home creates grave problems in bringing up children in Africa. Discipline may be difficult, since in Africa the father symbolizes authority in the family, and his prolonged absence from home may be felt deeply by family members. The mother, being overburdened by her many roles, may fail to play some, to the detriment of the development of the children.

The two-home phenomenon creates problems for the family in the way in which the family's resources are utilized. It is hard to consolidate resources when one has to divide them between two homes, for reasons stated above. The family thus lives in a quite unstable state, always hoping for some better home somewhere else. The psychological harm caused by such a state may be considerable. The children live and grow with no sense of belonging anywhere, neither to the town nor the country. This may create problems of identity for them, leading to delinquency or lack of purpose in life, a symptom which is now common among African youth.

Most Africans who migrate to towns often look forward to their eventual return to their rural homes. In most cases, this is done during old age or sickness. Thus, when a man realizes that he can no longer work in the town, he makes his journey home and joins his family from which he may have been separated for many years. This reunion tends to create much friction within the family, in particular, where the man has not been a regular visitor during his working days. The fact that the wife might have taken over some of his roles in his absence makes adjustment to his family rather difficult. For example, he may find that his wife is now used to making decisions by herself regarding the utilization of family property, the discipline of the children and the like. He may be faced with teenage children whom he may not be in a position to control, since he has not established any relationship with them. In most cases he may be faced with an undeveloped home with most of its inhabitants living below the poverty line. Faced with all these problems, the man may engage in adjustment techniques which often create more problems in the family. For example, it is quite common in Africa to find retired persons investing their hard-earned pensions in marrying other wives, abusing alcohol or investing money in very elaborate and expensive projects that do not succeed but manage to drain the family's meagre resources.

Extended family systems

Although the extended family system has been discussed in the section on marriage above, it deserves to be discussed on its own as it is an important feature of African life, with merits and demerits regarding the family. For many years the extended family has been a noble characteristic of African society especially at times of death, during disputes and in production and the upbringing of children. It was seen as a social security system on the continent.

At times of death, the children of the deceased were looked after by the extended family, often the uncles or aunts. The children brought into the household of relatives were treated equally with those of that household. This means that the children were given an equal chance to grow and develop and look after others in adulthood. When there were disputes in terms of marriages, land or inheritance, the members of the extended family participated in the reconciliation and, because they knew the family better, they were better judges of disputes than an outsider trying to resolve conflicts from a theoretical perspective. The members of the extended system participated in the production of what they consumed. This means that the resources were cared for, and, where they were scarce, preference was given to children and the aged. The children belonged to everybody in the system, and anybody of adult age in the system could discipline them. Hence children did not look only to parents for discipline and protection. The parents on the other hand, were not allowed to neglect their responsibilities through habits like abusing alcohol. The father was expected to provide for and protect his family, and, where he abused alcohol to the detriment of the family, the members of the extended family had the right to reprimand him. On the other hand, the mother was expected to look after her family well, her husband included, and, where she failed, her husband had the right to marry another wife.

Although Africa has been changing, the extended family system is still very much alive, although it has been changing in its functions. Its members still expect to be looked after by the fortunate members of the family. Thus if one member works, he is expected to look after the entire family. For example, statements like 'Your success is also ours' are quite common. The system worked very well during the time of subsistence economy when support was derived basically from the land. With the onset of a cash economy, the system posed plenty of problems to the family Although few people in Africa participate in the cash economy, the rest of the population expects to share the income since they are part and parcel of the system. In fact, in Africa, the majority of the rural population may not look to the state (government) for help nor expect the state to help them as a right, but they expect help to come from their relatives. It can be observed that in Africa political struggles are mainly for power (who rules) rather than for support, as the majority of the population still expect help to come from their relatives more than the state. Jobs, support, education, mobility and the like are still sought through the extended family network. This puts much strain on some family members, especially those who are better off in terms of education.

Other implications for the family include, for example, homicide, apathy, extravagance, large families, underdevelopment, lack of creativity, unnecessary conformity, feelings of irrelevance, petty jealousies and dependency. A man faced with an inability to support himself or his immediate family as well as other relatives may decide not to support anybody at all, and may indulge in practices of self-destruction like excessive drinking, gambling or refusing to work, as he sees no point in working if expectations are too high. Since his resources may be stretched too far, he may fail to improve his standard of living and remain in poverty or unfulfilled. Faced with too much pressure from relatives who are giving him different messages, he may find it difficult to make decisions, and thus become dependent and lack creativity. Because he may not like to be bothered by his relatives, he may decide to have many children, and may develop a sense of being irrelevant especially where family issues have to be discussed, simply because he is tired of everybody in the system seeking help from him.

On the other hand, the other members of the system, realizing that they are being isolated by their successful relatives, may develop hostility towards them. This is often shown through gossip, curses, unnecessary land disputes, homicide and witchcraft in Africa – all these forms of aggression being directed at the relative who is denying them their extended family right not only to have a share in but also to influence the spending of the relative's income. In most parts of Africa these squabbles thwart the individual's initiative and creativity and interfere with his efficiency. Hence, the extended family system that used to support families in times of need has in some ways become destructive of the African family. At times of death, for example, some members of the family system look forward to the family property like land, houses, cars, clothes, money and cattle rather than taking into consideration the children of the family. Once they have distributed the deceased's property, they seem to want to have nothing to do with the deceased's family.

Polygamy

Polygamy has been widely practised in Africa, and it had important functions. For example, in situations where the wife could not have children, the husband could marry another wife. Besides, the African man tended to enjoy having many wives as it was a measure of wealth. The African man did not only value variety, but he also needed many people to work on his land, and marrying many wives satisfied this need.

Although one would expect that polygamy created many conflicts among the wives, it acted as a safety valve for handling marital squabbles between a husband and the wives. It created a situation where women could rotate around the husband. This arrangement must have been extremely therapeutic for the African man, so that even if he was impulsive or aggressive, his impulse was well cared for and there was no need to show his aggression. The impression is that the African remained rather neutral in this relationship, and he was able to delegate his powers according to the seniority of the wives. He was able to allow the wives considerable freedom to decide where to stay. For example, the wives could even have their own homesteads if they found it hard to live in one homestead. Whatever the circumstances, the economic situation at that time enabled him to build each wife a house, and so each woman handled her own household.

Many African men remained polygamous, and, although, the economic situation may not favour such an arrangement, they still have the tendency to marry more than one wife. Western education and religion have not discouraged them, and one still finds even the most educated man still opting for many wives. The present trend is to marry a second wife without consulting the first wife at all, although she is expected to share the house with the new wife.

At other times, especially in towns a man may spend nights away, possibly with another woman, about whom he is in two minds as to marriage. He may even raise children outside his marriage either with or without his wife's knowledge. In certain situations, the man associates with very young girls, and he sometimes dates young schoolgirls. He may bring girl friends to his wife's house, and demand that the wife leave the bed. All these practices can reflect the polygamous nature of the African man and his struggle consciously or unconsciously to maintain the practice.

Such behaviour tends to create problems for the family and contributes to most family instability in Africa today. In the process of acquiring the second wife, the family often suffers because family resources are largely wasted in other forms of extra-marital relations. Often, especially in the towns, the children hardly see their father, who appears to be too much involved gratifying his immediate needs. The mother, very much left to her own resources in this process, develops hostility towards the children, as most of the time she is expected to be with them.

Lack of space in towns makes polygamy rather irksome for the children of the household. Although, in certain situations, the man insists that his first wife/wives go and stay in their rural homes, often the wives reject the request, especially when they are employed and have some income. Because most men cannot afford to acquire independent accommodation for newly married wives, often everybody stays in one house and children go through hard times. Not only do they experience and witness constant quarrels between the wives, but they witness the double standards which leave them with many unanswered questions. For example, they may see that their neighbour has only one wife, and, when they go to church or school, the Christian style of living is stressed, and yet their own father has brought in another woman whom they are supposed to regard as a mother.

To most urban African children, a person called a 'mother' is that one who has given birth to you. The African traditional mother does not fit in with the English concept of a mother. Yet, their father would expect the children to regard the new wife as a mother and to call her such while their own mother was still alive and lived in the same house. All this creates much conflict not only in the family but in the children, and may explain alcohol and drug abuse among the youth in Africa. In situations where a father has been very concerned about his children (family) and suddenly he acquires another wife and denies his children the love and the care he used to give them, the children have suffered tremendously. For example, some have manifested their frustration through suicide attempts while others have broken down and ended up in psychiatric hospitals.

This happens because, furthermore, the children are never prepared or consulted about the new member of the family. Besides, often privileges are withdrawn suddenly, and the children are left wondering what wrong they have done to their father to require such punishment. Most of these marriages tend to take place when the children are either approaching their teenage years or when they are really teenagers and need their parental support and guidance to go through the turmoils of adolescence. The situation becomes worse when the new wife in the household starts to have her own children. In most cases the father of the house tends to favour these new arrivals over his earlier children. Sometimes the father considers these children to be better children than those of his first wife. In fact, in Africa, a man tends to love his children according to how he loves the mother. Thus, the mother that is loved most is advantaged in that her children are also loved and will be cared for by the husband. This may explain the phenomenon in polygamous homes in Africa that children of first wives sometimes tend to do poorly and hence are less successful compared to children of other wives.

Polygamous marriages have not only created problems for the children, but for the women as well. In traditional Africa when a man married another wife, the first wife did not see it as her fault, because polygamy was normal by all the standards at that time. With the coming of Christianity and subsequent education and so-called civilization, the African woman has been exposed to Western marriage where emphasis is put on love and one wife – 'until death do us part'. It then becomes very demoralizing when an African woman of today learns that her husband has acquired or is in the process of acquiring another wife. 'One flesh' not only becomes two different persons, but one person moves and merges with another flesh and the first wife is left alone. The state is not only humiliating but frightening. Since the first wife is often not consulted, she is left to draw her conclusions as to reasons that might have led her husband in modern Africa to marry another wife. Unless he is a Muslim, the wife often has no alternative but to blame herself. She concludes that the husband might have married another wife because she is insufficiently educated, not presentable, a poor partner, a bad wife, a bad mother and so on. All these reasons are often thrown up at her, and lead to feelings of guilt and depression. This is often manifested with the development of prolonged illnesses like permanent headaches that respond to no doctor's medicine, possession of spirits, excessive use of African medicine, especially charms or love medicines, frequent visits to witch doctors, attempted suicide, homicide and the like. All this is aimed at winning back the husband's love. While all this is happening the children also suffer and not only experience physical hardships, but emotional deprivation as well, as the parents are too much engrossed in their own problems. Such experiences may harm the children, especially when they have to start playing adult roles, and bode ill for future marriages and parenting in African families. Already results can be seen in the high separation and divorce rates that have been on the increase in Africa.

Polygamy has also been experienced where a family has been working very hard for years and has managed to save enough, hoping that life might be better for the family in old age. After wealth has been accumulated, the man decides to marry other women, leading to its dispersal. After years of saving, the family has to start all over again. The man, in turn, starts bringing up young children in his old age, and is not sure how they will manage in the future. With the money economy that has been penetrating Africa, often these children (especially sons) do not only face problems of identity, as their father is often too old to identify with, but they may also end up with no education. Often they join the unemployed and dependent groups rotating from one relative to the next for support, a phenomenon common in Africa. Thus polygamy which has in the past been a noble practice in Africa may create untold conflicts in the African families of today, leading to family instability.

The working mother

Although this section deals mainly with mothers in urban areas who are employed or self-employed, it is important that mothers who work on the rural farms are briefly discussed.

The woman tending her farm and home in the absence of her husband often faces problems of decision-making. It is a fact that most of rural farming is done by women in Africa. Yet when it comes to decisions regarding the sale of crops, cattle and the utilization of the income from the farms or other business ventures in rural Africa, the man has to decide. The woman cannot sell a piece of land or cattle to pay school fees for her children without informing her husband. If the husband refuses, then she sacrifices her children's education to please the husband. Sometimes after the sale of the crops, the woman hands over all the money she has earned to her husband, who in turn may use it for drink and entertaining his friends or marrying another wife. Most men can scarcely bring themselves to use the money to improve the living standard of the family, let alone thank the woman who has worked so hard and sacrificed much to earn it. All these contradictions lead to many squabbles in families and may end up with suicide and untold sufferings by the rural woman.

The working mother in the urban areas in Africa faces unique problems. Firstly, in order to go and work she has to have someone to look after her house or children while she is away the whole day, and Africans are familiar with the concept of houseboys and housegirls. The working mother, who works either to support herself and the family or to supplement her husband's income, may not be in a position to employ a qualified houseboy or maid. Hence, the tendency is either to bring some young relatives from the rural communities to help or to employ young boys and girls in the house. Many problems are experienced with the arrangement. The children left under the care of these young helpers may not only be physically and sexually molested, but husbands may also take advantage of the young maids and sexually exploit them. There are even certain situations in which the husband may marry a maid. The outcome, however, is that the working mother's marriage stands at risk of dissolution, and her children may be abused in her absence.

Another problem area for a working mother is how the money she earns from her work is to be utilized, especially where both partners are working. Few African men discuss their earnings with their wives. This means that at times the wife may not even know how much her husband is making. While this is the case, the husband may demand to know or be given her salary. In certain situations the husband buys everything with her money and the wife must be content with his choice. At times part of this money is used to support the husband's family, but the wife cannot use it to support her family if the husband has paid the bride-wealth. Once the dowry is paid, the wife is not expected to support her family, and whatever she earns in marriage is considered to belong to the husband. This attitude creates problems in the families especially where the wife feels exploited as she has no say about what she earns.

In certain situations, especially where the husband and the wife have joint bank accounts, the wife may be shocked to learn that her husband has mismanaged all the money earned and saved. This leads to the setting up of separate bank accounts, and each party may end up spending their earnings on whatever they like. This creates problems in the family as the children may sometimes remain insufficiently supported, although both parents may be working. In general, the way money is used in African families tends to generate conflict. Saving becomes difficult since both partners seem not to trust each other. This leads to wastage of the usually scarce resources. There are some provocative situations where the husband takes all the money the wife earns in order to marry another wife. Sometimes he demands that his first wife supports the other wives if she has to continue working after his marriage to the other wives. In these ways, family problems multiply.

Most women who work in urban areas in Africa play multiple roles. They are expected to be homemakers and child rearers as well as holding jobs in offices or other places of work. The working woman expects, in fact, to combine family and housewifely activities with regular employment. Unless there is mutual agreement by the couples regarding roles in marriage, these expectations conflict and may create problems for the working woman. This is so especially when the wife comes from work in the evening tired, and yet the husband expects her to play the role of mother and wife with maximum efficiency. In most cases, African men are not expected to help with housework, and the wife is expected to perform her motherly duties as soon as she arrives home. Even in situations where there is a helper or helpers in the house, the helpers tend to be reluctant to work as soon as the mother arrives home. The helpers actually expect her to take over, because work outside home, especially in offices or where mental ability is being used, is not considered to be tiring. The husband who arrives home soon leaves to socialize with his menfriends in bars or clubs after taking tea. The wife is left at home to look after the children, cooking for them, making sure that they eat and sending them to bed. She then waits to open the door to her husband and gives him food. The return of the husband from bars or clubs is often unpredictable, and it could be at any time from 9 p.m. to 2 a.m. Some men even cause problems if the wife is not available to receive them. Some demand that the wives wake up and sit up for them while they are eating, and failure to do so may lead to wife-beating.

The wife for the most part has to wake up very early in order to make sure that warm water is available for the husband's bath and that the children are prepared for school. Thus, the work the woman does after her office work is indeed stressful. In most cases she does this with either no support or minimal support from the helper. Weekends are equally frustrating, as the wife ends up managing her household duties single-handed and hardly rests at all. Sometimes her situation is made worse by relatives who may flock to the house and choose to be waited on. The woman's situation is made more difficult because in Africa visitors do not make appointments for visits: she may find herself with many visitors at weekends when she would prefer to be resting. Besides, the husband may also decide to bring his friends home without informing his wife. All these visitors expect not only to be welcomed but also served with food. The wife who resents all this is considered selfish or a bad wife. In these ways it can be seen that the working couples in Africa are now creating stress in the family; for the African woman the demands of holding a job outside home are not compatible with what she is expected to offer to her family, relatives and friends at home. Although in her office job she may have to perform all the duties performed by men, her home duties are really those of a 'good African woman' – that is, one who keeps her household together, runs it efficiently, brings up the children, and welcomes anybody home with a wide smile on her face, and also produces sons and daughters as God may allow.

Conflict management

The management of the problems discussed in the foregoing section are discussed in two parts – namely, the traditional and the Western approaches.

The traditional approaches to conflict management

In Africa, every community has its own way of handling problems that may affect the family and that are likely to lead to its dissolution. None the less, there were various techniques that were widely used and are still being used in some parts of Africa to help solve some of the family problems. For example, avoidance and joking relationships have been widely used in Africa mainly to prevent problems occurring among family members. In situations where girls and boys were considered mature enough to have babies, they were not allowed to be alone with their parents – especially girls were not allowed to be near their fathers. The rules were even more strict once they got married. Neither of the married spouses were allowed to interact with their parents-in-law. In some cultures, they were not allowed even to shake hands. For example, in some cultures it was taboo for a daughter-in-law to open the door of her parents-in-law's house. The daughters and sons-in-law sat with their parents-in-law only on special occasions. If the parents wished to talk to the couple, messages might be sent through the daughter or the son. Such arrangements helped to reduce the conflict that would have arisen had the parties been allowed to interact freely.

The joking relationships were for the most part limited between brothers and sisters-in-law and the grandparents. Such easy relationships allowed for the development of trust, and when one had a problem, it was easier for one to seek help from the relative with whom he was allowed to joke. The joking relationships also helped create an effective way of communication between families. For example, in marriage, the couples knew exactly what they were expected to do when an aunt or a sister or a brother made a certain remark. A lazy woman hearing her brother-in-law making a joking statement like 'I wasted my cows for nothing' would get the message clearly and evaluate herself in relation to the statement. In most cases she would take the hint, and this prevented a problem that might have followed the undesired behaviour. Hence, the jokes were not only therapeutic but preventive as well.

When the family lost the breadwinner, as on the death of a father, it was often not allowed to disintegrate, as one of the brothers, cousins or any relative of the father was nominated to look after the home. This brought about the concept of 'widow inheritance' in Africa. Here the widow was married to the husband's relative. The wife was compelled to stay in the clan and was not allowed to take away the children of the deceased. The man who inherited her was supposed to look after her and her children and any children fathered in the association. This arrangement facilitated family stability after death and created homeostasis within the family. The children managed to grow up with few problems. Where both parents died, the children of the household were looked after by uncles, aunts or other relatives. The children, for the most part, had equal rights just like other children, and whatever their parents left in terms of property was given to them as their birthright. In fact, one could consider this arrangement as informal fostering where the children were looked after by the relatives, but they still retained their father's name and land. The children of a dead person were never mistreated in

Africa, as there was a general belief that the spirit of a dead person is very much alive and may see all that happens to the children. For this reason mistreatment was seen as a situation that might bring about family misfortune. Therefore, for a long time there have been kinship obligations in Africa and most people adhered to them.

In situations where there have been marital problems between couples, often the equivalent of group counselling was practised in Africa. The wife went to her parents, or brothers in the absence of parents, and reported her marital problems. Often she was calmed down, and told to go back to her husband and children and see whether the situation improved. If the problem persisted after the individual counselling by the mother or sister-in-law or even father, the wife would probably go back to her parents and refuse to return to her husband until her husband came to her home for an open discussion. The husband often cooperated, and went for discussion taking with him either his father, brother and uncle or a friend or any other relative in whom he had some trust. The wife was also represented by her parents or relatives.

At the conference the guests were made to relax by being offered food and drink. After this, the wife was asked by her uncle or mother to state her problems. The husband was then given an opportunity to respond to the allegations. Facts were often weighed, and whoever seemed to be in the wrong was openly warned. If the situation was too grave, like frequent beatings, lack of respect and support, often the parents of the wife demanded some payment before releasing the woman back to her husband. The open discussions helped quite a lot to stabilize marriages and created a bond between the families. Some husbands avoided unnecessary conflicts as they feared the confrontation with their parents-in-law. In fact both parties were helped to identify their weak points in marriage, and were bluntly asked to improve on those points. When it was realized that the wife really caused the problem and would not change her behaviour, especially where she abused alcohol, the husband was advised to marry another wife, and the first wife's behaviour was tolerated.

There were situations where a woman or a man had emotional conflicts caused by a poor relationship in marriage. For example, where a man had married another wife because his first wife could not have children or could not bear sons, often the wife grew depressed and became mute or developed some hysterical behaviour. She might claim to have been possessed by spirits and run away from home. Then the family would consult a witch doctor, and sacrifices would be made mainly to drive the spirits out of her. The technique and the process were indeed therapeutic, as from the moment of the treatment, the woman not only obtained support and attention from the witch doctor, but also drew her husband's attention away from the new wife. For that moment she became the centre of attention; she managed to control her husband and any other significant person in her life, and when there was a response from these people she would recover from her illness after several sacrifices had been made.

The above methods of handling conflicts are still very much used in rural Africa.

The western approaches to conflict management

Western techniques of handling family problems have been filtering into Africa and are mainly concentrated in the urban areas. The rural African does not have the advantage of these services, and, although changing, the traditional methods are still used to some extent.

The first western method to be introduced was counselling, and individuals with problems concerning living in families were seen and helped to resolve their problems. Counselling was mostly done by priests and missionaries trained in marriage counselling and guidance in the West. The early counsellors were concerned with helping Christians with marital problems as well as helping with career selection. In general, the concern was with good Christian living and marriage. With the introduction of social work in Africa, another form of counselling emerged. This was casework, a personal service provided by trained workers for individuals who require skilled assistance in resolving some material, emotional or personality problem. The caseworker is supposed to use counselling techniques to help the client deal with his problems in order to achieve a better adjustment with his environment. Casework remains an individualized service and is concerned with social as well as personal factors; with change in the environment as well as in the individual; with mobilizing community resources as well as with personal resources. The assumption is that casework does not only help the individual but the society as well. None the less, casework is concerned primarily with the development and adjustment of the individual rather than the societal arrangements. The principles used are acceptance, self-responsibility and confidentiality. All these facilitate the development of rapport between the case worker and the client.

The worker is expected to accept the client irrespective of the client's behaviour or conduct. Hence, the worker develops a non-judgemental attitude although he may not condone the client's conduct. Believing in self-responsibility, the worker observes that the client has the right to make his own decision to accept the services offered; the worker sees this as a beginning of the development of independence on the part of the client. One of the aims of case work is to help the client resume his responsibilities as soon as possible. Because the caseworker sees confidentiality as the fundamental right of the client the client's information has to be protected, and no information obtained by the worker should be revealed to anybody without the client's consent. Moreover, all reports and files on the case must be safely kept so that nobody can have access to them. The worker is at all times aware of the limitations of these principles and modifies his approach according to the situation.

As can be seen from the above, casework prepares the individual to fit into his environment, and the environment is manipulated only in order to facilitate the individual's adjustment to it. Because of this individualized approach, some workers offering counselling services to families realize its limitations and group counselling has been introduced under different titles. One that is most commonly being introduced into some large African towns is family therapy. The assumption here is that the individual presenting a problem for help may actually be presenting the family problem, and he may not be the only person affected in the family feud. This approach calls for all the family members to be included in the treatment depending on their age, with young children being excluded.

The family members are brought together in order to make a diagnosis of the family problem. The worker or the therapist is concerned with communication patterns in the family and how the roles are being played. When the parents are found to have marital problems, the children are released from the treatment and the parents are seen alone. This approach has claimed much success in the West, and is closely related to the way in which Africans traditionally handled family problems, as already discussed. None the less, the degree of family therapy's success has still to be measured in Africa, since the few therapists practising it are meeting resistance from the husbands. Although it requires that both parents participate in the treatment, often fathers or husbands are unwilling to go and discuss family problems with an outsider. In casework, because of this lack of cooperation, the case workers concentrate their efforts on material help and often deal only with the person presenting the problem. Occasionally, they meet the father or husband, only to try to alert him to the problem. In family therapy, the therapist does not put emphasis on material help, but concentrates on family relationships. Although it is in its early stages in Africa, this approach would be the most effective way of handling family problems in general.

Apart from the above approaches, there are other forms of treatment aimed at helping communities in general. It was hoped that if communities were organized, problems affecting families might be prevented. This approach is known as community work. In rural areas community work takes the form of community development, whereas in towns there is community organization.

Community development is designed to improve the economic, social and cultural conditions of communities through the active participation of local residents. In the process, the family is implicitly helped, as communities consist of families. The movement goes through phases. Resources have been mobilized and created by self-help groups, and it is well known that schools, health centres, community centres, churches and houses have been built through the movement. At the moment, income-generating activities are being emphasized, all aimed at improving family welfare.

Community organization is concerned with setting up social welfare services in the urban areas. The work is mainly done by non-governmental organizations like Christian councils of social service, relief organizations and the like. The activities are centred on inter-organizational coordination and service development in the towns. Families have benefited from such movements because some counselling services have been established through community organizations.

Finally, various types of institutions have been established in urban areas in Africa to cater for family members who find difficulty in living in the family system. For example, children who need care and protection and those with behaviour problems are sometimes taken to approved schools. Those children who lose their parents and end up having nobody to look after them are often taken to children's homes or foster homes, or they are adopted. In situations where the parents have failed adequately to play their roles, the children are either placed under foster care or taken to children's homes. Africa is now familiar with Dr Barnardo's and S.O.S. children's homes. When parents grow old with no one to support them, there are homes for the aged where such people can stay until they die, although such homes are very rare. In fact, in certain African countries there are now organizations looking at the problems of single parents, battered wives and physically abused children.

Although these services are indeed scattered and inadequate for the demand, one can conclude that their development, although slow, is in fact following the Western trend. The pace at which Western models are being copied is really fast, a situation that needs to be looked into seriously, as there is very little one can call an African approach to handling conflicts in urban Africa.

5 Areas of family policy in Africa

Government family policy can be defined as the goals set by government for family well-being, or as achievements gained by government enactments on behalf of the family. Family policy varies a great deal depending on political and social systems, but basically it is concerned with family well-being. In most cases family policy is explicitly stated.

Explicit family policy includes those particular policies and programmes designed to achieve or realize specified goals regarding the family. These may include child welfare, family counselling services, family planning, income maintenance, tax rebates, housing policies, day-care centres and the like. Here the family is clearly the object of such government policies.

By contrast, implicit family policy includes the accidental, implied or unanticipated consequences of policies designed to accomplish very different objectives, but the family ends up being affected. Such policies may be related to industrial locations, road building, the building of estates, trade and tariff regulations, migration and immigration rules and many other enactments. Here the purposes or intentions of the family policy may be latent or indeed unintended.

The concept of family policy originated in the Western world where, in certain situations, the family was either becoming so disintegrated that it bordered on extinction or so stable that no force could interfere with its existence. Whatever view taken, the approach created problems for the development of family policies in the West, and the distinction between family policy and other types of social and economic policy is not entirely clear. For example, in the United States, it seems that because the family is seen as a private institution and thus not to be interfered with, public assistance is given only when necessary and the state does not need to interfere with private arrangements. On the other hand, because Britain sees the family as capable of being destroyed by a number of forces it has decided that it must be protected by means of public assistance policies, leading Britain to become a welfare state. The above distinctions are not really mutually exclusive, but they create problems for developing countries in policy-making related to the family, as it is hard to decide which model to use.

The African situation

The concept of family policy is relatively new in Africa, and wherever a type of policy exists, it is modelled on the Western style. However, as already stated, family policies throughout the world show great variation, and African nations have a problem in selecting which one to follow. This may partly explain the fact that, where there are family policies in Africa, they tend not to be specific and comprehensive. In fact, some African countries have not even seen the need to have family policies and reason that the solution to social problems can be left to traditional methods until such time as economic progress has improved the living standard of the people. Although the problem of lack of resources in African countries must be acknowledged, the various social problems that accompany changing patterns of family life are new and cannot be left to traditional methods of handling them as these methods are in fact fast disappearing.

Because of the economic and social situations that prevail in Africa, most African states tend to see families as beneficiaries of economic and social development. Only a few states consider families as potential resources in such programmes. Therefore, one can conclude that most family policies in Africa are implicit or accidental rather than explicitly stated – which is understandable and unavoidable considering that much of Africa is still rural and illiterate, with few or undeveloped resources. Even social or public policies tend to be made haphazardly. For example, when there is a national crisis (political upheavals tend to be endemic) or an economic crisis, policies tend to emerge from nowhere regarding, say, citizenship, children's education, economic measures or employment indicating that African nations are not at all systematic in working out necessary policies, whether family, social, economic or political. Even the Western model used seems to depend on the considerations of a particular moment, leading to the confusion of concepts or goals. This in turn leads to duplication of programmes and activities geared at accomplishing policies.

Types of family policy in Africa

There are limitations in listing types of family policy prevalent in Africa as such a list will not only fail to describe adequately the real African situation, but will also somewhat resemble a Western list. In addition, distinctions must be drawn between urban and rural situations, a venture that may complicate family policies in Africa even more. Above all, different African states tend to use models from the Western world relative to their colonial and Western experiences. This makes it rather difficult to talk of family policies in Africa. None the less, the following areas of concern and legislation may be identified: social welfare measures; family allowances; special family services; social security; legal provisions; public housing; employment and population policy. These are discussed below.

Social welfare measures

These vary a great deal in Africa. In some countries, they are seen as remedial measures, while in others they are seen as both preventive and developmental measures. Where they are considered remedial, the emphasis is put on the disadvantaged members of the society, but where they are considered preventive and developmental the emphasis is on the development of human resources leading to national development.

The first social welfare measures were introduced into Africa by the colonial governments. They were mainly based on and related to the Christian religion, and their provision rested almost entirely on humanitarian feelings. The measures were charity-oriented, remedial in character, piecemeal and disjointed. They consisted of simple community facilities; relief services during calamities and emergencies; restriction of beggars, delinquency, vagrancy and major social evils.

The measures took a long time to be accepted as an integral part of national development plans since the immediate benefits were difficult to measure. The programmes were seen to be the responsibility of voluntary organizations, as the following statement indicates:

. . . While Governments address themselves to major services such as Social Security, Income Maintenance, Public Health, Education, Employment and Enforcement of Law etc., the services to underprivileged individuals and groups and other residual services could be undertaken by voluntary bodies (Tessema, 1971:11).

Although the situation described above has not changed much and social welfare measures remain remedial programmes for the unfortunate members of society, there is a general realization and acceptance of the fact that social welfare measures are relevant to the development of human resources, a pre-condition for national development. As such most African nations have included social welfare measures in their national development plans. Although they appear vague and sometimes too general, the move is none the less positive and may lead to more clearly specified family policies.

Social welfare measures include family welfare programmes with the primary purpose of strengthening the unity and integrity of the family; child welfare, which can be seen in the programmes of maternal and child health clinics and day care programmes; youth welfare services, intended mainly to initiate youths into adult roles and to prepare them for future responsibilities; and institutional care for children in need of care and protection.

Unfortunately the above-mentioned programmes are for the most part concentrated in the urban areas, especially in the African big cities, and their presence is hardly felt in the rural communities. These measures seem to give a false impression that while the urban family in Africa is changing, the rural family remains intact.

Family allowances

In some situations these are known as assistance programmes for the family. They include programmes such as income-tax relief, awarded mainly to working parents and to that parent with the highest income. In other situations we have free primary education, subsidized school meals, social security and other insurance measures, relief systems and wage plans.

All the above measures, apart from free education and subsidized school meals, tend to favour the individuals who are employed or working. Since unemployment is a problem in Africa, most families in Africa do not benefit from the programmes, merely admiring their existence. The situation is even worse in the rural areas, where the people are not only not covered under the schemes but may not even know of their existence.

The allowances as they stand now are too few, and some may not only be irrelevant to the African situation, such as programmes for relief of distress and hospital insurance, but may have actually encouraged malpractice. For example, giving of food or money may not only create dependency but are also demoralizing to the recipient, as it confirms to him that he is disadvantaged or useless. Claims for hospital insurance are sometimes demeaning and encourage corruption. Besides, the hospitals for which one is allowed to claim are too few and are concentrated in the towns. In the rural areas there are almost no hospitals where hospital insurance cards can be used, and thus it remains a programme for the advantaged group.

Where there is free primary education, the family still faces problems, as there are yet other expenses that the family has to face – for example, they must subscribe to building funds and pay for uniforms and so on. Furthermore, free education, for the most part, is not based on the family income, so that even those who can afford are also given free education. Secondary education, on the other hand, is too expensive for the African who relies on the subsistence economy. This makes many children stop schooling after primary education. Secondary education must be improved in order to be useful to African families, as there are no explicitly stated policies concerning what to do with those children who have completed their primary education but cannot afford secondary education.

Special family services

These are special measures taken by African states to handle family problems, and are at times set out in the national development plans. They include family counselling services, family planning, maternity leave and the like.

Counselling services in Africa are not new, and traditionally family members have often counselled each other in situations where they faced problems in marriage, landownership or other family conflicts, as already stated in the last chapter. None the less, with social changes these services became formalized mainly to cater for urban problems. Counselling means different things to different countries. In certain situations the services have been individualized and only carried out by trained counsellors, who are few indeed. In others, the services have been too diluted, and may be used to teach family planning, good food or balanced diet, or better family living. All this has caused confusion not only among the practitioners, but also for those counselled.

So far, most counselling services have been concerned with women and children, and could hardly be considered of benefit to men. The families themselves have not seen the benefits of counselling and at times do not look for such services, a situation which has retarded their development. Besides, because counselling has not been seen as directly related to economic development, which is highly emphasized in developing countries, Africa included, counselling services are not seen as a priority in national planning and has remained a domain of voluntary organizations, which are mostly run by foreigners. This state of affairs has led to the commercialization of counselling services in some African countries, and it is not uncommon to see counselling advertised in the local papers.

The formalized nature of counselling seems not to have been recognized and accepted by Africans, and it is not uncommon to find untrained individuals claiming to be counsellors. Sometimes, because there are few trained counsellors, supervision becomes impossible which results in less qualified counsellors giving services. Often, these leave much to be desired in terms of the services they offer, thus discouraging people from seeking these services. All this makes counselling services appear to be a 'common-sense' service which anybody can give, rather than a professional provision which can be clearly stated in terms of national or family policies.

Another special family service that has penetrated Africa is family planning. Although covered below under population policy, it is important to make several observations about it. Family planning services have been introduced by voluntary organizations of foreign origin, and few African states have shown the enthusiasm of incorporating them into their programmes. Being an unacceptable service to most African states, different approaches have been used to make the programme acceptable. For example, too much emphasis has been put on the health of the women, associating family planning with women, instead of with youths or men. This may be responsible for the negative attitude African men have towards family planning methods.

The promoters of family planning in Africa have gone so far as to claim that family planning is not a new idea in Africa, as traditionally families were spaced. One is inclined to think that what might have appeared to be family planning was an accidental occurrence. For example, because in polygamous marriages there were many women to satisfy the man's sexual desires, and unions might have occurred when the wife was not fertile, the spacing of children appears to have been sheer chance with no planning involved.

The family planning services suffer the same problems that most services in Africa experience, in that they are concentrated in the urban areas. Country people have to travel long distances to find the services, and sometimes transportation, including fares, is a problem. Besides, in situations where some people may not get enough food to feed themselves, it would be expecting too much for them to sacrifice whatever they have for services they may not understand or for which they do not see immediate benefits.

Although social and economic programmes geared to families are limited in Africa, children are valued and looked upon as security systems in old age. Where pensions, insurance plans and other support systems are still rudimentary, it is hard to persuade people to have few children. Besides, where people are poor with very little hope of improving themselves, having many children may be considered an achievement. For these reasons, family planning services may take time to be accepted and may be seen both by the people and the planners as one of Africa's luxury services. Until the present time, it has remained a sensitive and controversial service in Africa.

Another area of interest is maternity services offered to working mothers. To rural mothers this service is a luxury, and most women in rural areas tend to go back to their duties as soon as possible. None the less, following the Western model of maternity services, African working women enjoy this service, and often the period ranges from 1 to 3 months depending on the mother's economic and marital status. Single mothers in most countries have to rush back to work in order to support themselves, whereas mothers from high-income groups can afford to stay at home for additional months without pay.

Although in the West mothers get some allowances during maternity leave such funds are not available in most African countries, and mothers have either to be content with their salaries or nothing (as with rural mothers). Maternity leave is usually for women, and men are scarcely involved at all. In most cases the men are expected to continue with their usual work unless special permission is obtained from the employer.

Social security

Social security can be defined as those measures taken by the state or society to provide medical care for all and to assure them of the means which are necessary in order to live decently in the event of loss or substantial reduction of their livelihood resulting from circumstances beyond their control. The methods and techniques used to accomplish these purposes are many, and vary from one state to another. They may include health insurance, a pension for retirement, accident insurance, unemployment benefits and the like. Some can be compulsory, whereas others are voluntary insurance schemes. The state may also provide public services under the social security system. In addition legal obligations may be imposed on the individual employer to bear the insurance costs.

Social security systems in industrialized nations have been seen as preventing social risks, compensation for loss of income in case of an accident, and help in returning to a normal way of life in society. The central pillar of the concept has been income compensation, which affects the majority of the population drawing a regular income. This orientation has little relevance to the African situation where the great majority of the people are not employed in the formal sector. Most Africans still live within the subsistence economy. Africa can still be seen in terms of two populations in one society – that is, a small minority with a regular income but nothing to fall back on when it is lost; and the vast majority with hardly any income at all, but an extended family and tribal structures, which are actually changing (as described earlier), to care for the members in need.

Traditionally, social security measures consisted of collective solidarity through mutual assistance within the family, clan and tribe. As already pointed out in previous chapters, members of the extended family looked after one another in times of crisis or old age. Besides, everybody contributed to the growing of whatever food they consumed.

Social change has been penetrating Africa, and during foreign rule in Africa some elements of social security schemes were introduced. Hence, social security existed but on a very limited scale at independence. African social security systems have been influenced by the Western view that the essential function of social security should be the protection of persons most affected by the process of development – that is, the emerging wage-earning class, with social security acting as a stabilizing factor in rapidly changing social conditions. This approach has lost sight of the groups most affected since these groups have not been explicitly identified. Foreign influence, moreover, is clearly manifested in the divergence of approaches to the techniques of social security administration in Africa. For example, in French-speaking Africa, social security schemes are implemented through pension insurance funds, whereas in those countries with British influence they are known as provident fund schemes. In short, the development of social security programmes in Africa is based on the historical, political and socio-economic background of each country.

The administration of social security schemes in Africa has not been easy for various reasons. First, the scheme seems to be viable only in situations where the majority of the people are employed or have cash income – essentially, a patching up service. Most people are still poor, and governments have to look for alternative ways of helping them. Second, the populations involved have little education and hence no concept of compulsory saving, and therefore may not see the need of letting part of their salary be deducted for vague services. Third, the extended family support system still exists in Africa, and most people who live in the urban areas still have kinship ties with the rural communities. In these circumstances, the minority who are involved in wage-earning must still support the majority, and with very little income. This reality, where resources have to be stretched beyond means, makes saving difficult for the African family. Besides, some people come to towns just to earn a little money for some special purpose in the rural areas; these needs may range from marriage to buying a piece of land or building a house in the rural community. Such an individual may work only for the length of time he feels will enable him to earn enough money – several months or, maybe, several years. To him the social security arrangement may not be useful at all, especially considering that pensions are available only at a certain age. Even hospital insurance may be unnecessary, since he may not fall ill during his brief period of work, and to enrol in a scheme would merely deprive him of his hard-earned money. This point illustrates the fact that most social security schemes are started without determining the real needs of the people. Their introduction seems to satisfy the needs of the planners rather than the receivers.

Although most social security systems in Africa are still in their formative stages, quite a number of African states have seen them to be related to economics rather than social or family policies. This led Vladimir Rys, when addressing the Fifth African Regional Conference of the International Social Security Association in 1974, to make the following statement:

> It also serves to show that those who tend to see in members of society only factors of production, forgetting that the well-being of these same members also happens to be the ultimate objective of all economic activities, do only part of their job (Rys, 1975:25).

In conclusion, social security measures in Africa, although aimed at protecting the persons most affected by the process of development, still suffer from many problems. These problems are related to the fact that we are trying to model services which are indeed only appropriate to a small section of the African population. Thus, one must analyse the needs of the vast majority of the population living off the proceeds of the land, and it seems that any attempt to extend income benefits to the African rural population must be based on new and unconventional methods. The social security systems of the Western world are indeed alien to the African situation, and may create problems rather than solve them.

Legal provisions

In Africa, a married woman has a right to be maintained or be provided with necessities by her husband. Where this duty is not discharged, especially in monogamous marriages, the woman automatically has the right to sue him for separation and maintenance. If the husband is found guilty, he may be imprisoned for a maximum of three years. The wife, on the other hand, seems not to have any corresponding duties regarding her treatment of the husband. However, her duties to the man are actually socially defined, whereas his duties to her are legally defined. The law makes it a man's burden to care for his wife, a situation that most African men loathe. And it causes the African woman to suffer in silence, as she realizes that society does not expect her to accuse her husband in court and that to do so may make her lose face among her friends. For these reasons she sacrifices her legal rights to meet societal expectations. Nevertheless, this arrangement tends to confirm women's lower status in society.

In Africa, where the law is intended to protect both husband and wife, the legal system does not provide tangible or workable enforcement procedures. For example, in Christian marriages most legal systems state that during the course of a legally binding marriage, either party is prohibited from contracting another marriage with someone other than the spouse. If this happens, the offender commits the crime of bigamy, and the offender may earn some years' sentence in gaol. This particular law is most often broken by African men, yet few are convicted, and so this law becomes ineffective. It seems that for the bigamy laws to be properly enforced, the legal systems in Africa will have to provide ways and means of deterring the African man's behaviour. In fact, in the few cases which have been taken to courts, the judges, who are the products of African and not of Western culture, tend not to reproach the criminal husbands, and there are many incidents to support this observation. However, whenever a husband takes the wife to court for infidelity, much publicity is given to the case and the man may end up getting his divorce even if the wife vehemently denies the allegation.

Another area of law where women still experience hardship is related to property ownership. For an African married woman to own any property, she has to consult her husband, unless she decides to have her own secret dealings, which may not be compatible with her conscience. Before the married woman is granted any loans she has to show that she has the consent of her husband, yet married men are not subjected to similar treatment, although there are differences in each country and among different religious groups. In certain cases women are given more power in relation to property ownership. For example, in some countries in West Africa women tend to enjoy equal status with men, though this is rare among women in East Africa.

Another area of discontent with regard to family laws in Africa is related to children, especially to custody and guardianship rules. Children, for the most part, are regarded as the property of parents in Africa. With hardly any public assistance, especially in old age, parents actually see children as insurance policies, and the decision as to who should have custody or guardianship becomes a problem where marriages have to be dissolved. Even after the courts have decided on the parent who will have custody, the other parent continues to interfere and children are pulled between the parents. Where the law decides that the father shall maintain his children while they live with their mother, often the father absconds, abandoning his responsibility, and the children end up suffering. Children born out of wedlock are often not well represented in African legal systems. Either they are illegally supported by their putative fathers (that is, the fathers secretly pay for their maintenance) or they are not supported at all, as the law does not provide for them in some African countries. The law, on the other hand, seems to be silent on ways and means of deterring both men and women from acquiring illegitimate children.

In conclusion, Western types of legal systems in Africa have many omissions simply because the African population is still committed to customs, values and beliefs that may hinder the enforcement of Western laws. This calls for constant reviews and the establishment of policies that may facilitate the reinforcement of those laws.

Public housing

Most African states have housing policies which are stated in national development plans. In most cases these are concerned with housing problems in the urban areas, leaving rural housing as an individual venture. Urban housing is often provided under different schemes. Some are for low-income groups, while others are intended for middle- and high-income groups.

Housing policies in Africa are influenced by Western housing policies, and it is believed that certain kinds of people or families should be given priority. However, because in some countries housing programmes are sometimes commercialized, at times they end up in the wrong hands. This leads to the concentration of houses in the hands of wealthier people, a situation that jeopardizes the government's good intentions.

Because the rate of population increase in the urban areas tends to defeat the best of housing programmes, housing remains a problem in most African towns. The scarcity makes the cost of houses in some African countries too high relative to the income of the majority of the people. The type of houses built in Africa tend to be a Western structure which is designed for a nuclear family. Most houses are not meant for the African extended family, which makes living difficult in urban areas, as often a large extended family finds itself lacking space.

Because housing is a problem, most states in Africa encourage both public and private housing enterprises. This approach has created many problems for the development of houses in these countries. Since the individual developers expect quick returns from their investment, most houses built under such a scheme are often poorly constructed and very expensive indeed. Because of the lack of public resources, publicly built houses are often few and people scramble for them, a practice that leads to corruption and other malpractices. Often government officials allocate publicly built houses to themselves, their relatives and friends and not to those who may need them. Hence, the majority of the poor in the urban areas live in very poor conditions, and the situation has led to the development of slum areas, a familiar characteristic of most African towns. Most of the houses that are available for those in low-income brackets are not only too small in size but lack the essential facilities. Most people, especially from low-income groups, live in congested situations where facilities for disposing household refuse and human waste are often inadequate or not available.

These housing problems are exacerbated by the land policies in some African countries, where most land available is privately owned and at times sold at prices beyond the means of most African town dwellers. Land owned by the state is often not enough for the majority of urban residents, and again ends up in the hands of those with power and those responsible for the allocations.

In some African countries, programmes for low-cost housing best known as site and service schemes have been initiated. Here people mainly from low-income groups are helped to build houses by themselves through the World Bank or other loan systems. The people themselves are expected to participate in the building process in self-help groups. The problem with this scheme is that the houses are not only too small for the large African families, but the owners of the houses often rent them for commercial purposes rather than living in them. The reason often given is that they have to get money to pay back the bank loans. Although the authority concerned has advised them to rent one room for loan payment and occupy other rooms, most owners prefer to rent these houses and to live in slum conditions.

In conclusion, few people in Africa benefit from housing programmes. The housing schemes that are available do not take into consideration African life styles – that is, the extended family systems and polygynous marriages.

Employment

The employment policies of most African states are well stated in their respective national development plans and are sometimes known as labour market policies. Most of these policies are related to the formal rather than the informal sector of the economy, since the informal sectors are often unregulated. The influence of governments for the most part in the informal sector is indirect.

Usually, wages and conditions of employment are fixed by the African states through wage councils or other bodies assigned the responsibility. Wages are related to specific trades, industries or occupations. For the most part there seems to be flexibility and differences, depending on whether one is working in agriculture or industry. Minimum wages, therefore, tend to vary not only from one industry to another, but depend on whether the individual is living in the city or a town in the rural community or working in a farm in the rural areas. Hours of work, rest days, holidays, annual sick leave and other conditions of employment differ from one place to another. The multi-dimensional type of regulation may lead to distortion of incentives with adverse effects on horizontal labour mobility. Hence Africa is characterized by great wage differentials among the workers, and this may not foster occupational mobility. The differences are even wider, in terms of working hours, between those who work in the offices and those who work in the agricultural sector.

Measures regarding industrial relations also exist and have been influenced by post-independence developments. The early legislation on trade unions and labour disputes followed Western models. However, these have been reshaped in an effort to adapt to systems and institutions that have more relevance to African conditions. Unfortunately, these bargaining mechanisms have tended to be a blend of voluntarism and government concern for development and can hardly be said to represent the workers effectively. In certain situations industrial courts have been established to look into the interest of both the employer and the employees, but they deal with urban workers and hardly represent workers in rural areas at all, where, in consequence, conditions of work remain unimproved.

A variety of methods or techniques are used to inform people about the job opportunities in different countries. Most countries in Africa have formal employment services, mainly government-run offices providing free services for employers and workers. In addition, there are private agencies charging a fee and commission for job connections. The problem with these arrangements is, first, that the employment offices do not exist in all parts of the countries, especially rural areas, as they are concentrated in the capital cities. Second, even where they exist they are not effectively utilized, as the labour market seems to be an individual affair, and employers sometimes give jobs to their relatives or friends. Sometimes jobs are bought at great cost and qualifications may not count. In fact, the general rule of recruitment seems to be that jobs are available at the factory gates or through friends, relatives or factory personnel officers. Only a small percentage of persons obtain jobs through the formalized systems.

Organized in the way they are, the employment exchanges have not been successful in establishing a meaningful information programme regarding the employment market and at times jobs have to be advertised through local newspapers, which fail to reach the majority of the people, especially those in low-income groups and those living in rural areas.

In discussing employment policies in Africa, it is also necessary to look into employment problems in general. Employment has been seen to provide people with access to the material fruits of economic growth, and to provide satisfaction to those who are employed, but in Africa it has been realized that many people work long hours for very little and they are not any better off than those who are unemployed. This has led to the development of concepts of 'the working poor' in the urban areas.

With the advent of new productive technology, modern business organization and the distinction between rural and urban life, the problem of unemployment has emerged in Africa. However, it is rather difficult to define unemployment in Africa, as at one extreme, there are people openly seeking jobs in the towns, especially the cities, while at the other end there are nomadic tribes with problems of poverty rather than occupation. In between, there are those who are partially employed, who sometimes perform traditional tasks and family obligations and sometimes produce material objects or services for sale.

With knowledge of the above complexities, African states have worked out different measures to combat the problem of unemployment. Most states now realize that it is not enough to rely on rapid economic growth to combat unemployment, and most states have changed their focus to rural areas, where programmes have been started mainly to keep the rural population in one place. For example, there are programmes to improve small-scale farming, to start cooperative movements, and to start special rural development programmes; there are others for technical and vocational training, rural industrial development centres, irrigation schemes, and the development of specific skills in agriculture and commerce, and the like. Such measures have been seen as long-term employment programmes which could help alleviate unemployment, of benefit to the family indirectly.

In addition, short-term measures have been taken to relieve unemployment. These include the decentralization of services, tripartite agreements, Africanization programmes, national youth services, rural development (for example, provision of water and electricity), the abolition of taxes among the low-income groups, and the introduction of other taxes like sales tax for middle- and high-income groups, the promotion of small-scale enterprises, and many other programmes that vary from one country to another.

The limitations of these measures are many, but the obvious one is that most of them remain well set out in the national development plans without being implemented, often because of monetary reasons. Sometimes priorities are forgotten, and close observation of most national development plans in Africa reveals many contradictions as often there is hardly any continuity from one plan to the next. Moreover at times there seems to be an unfortunate disregard of the pre-requisites for individual productivity. For example, for a person to be economically productive in our rural communities, he needs land to cultivate, sufficient education and training, and access to credit and technical knowledge. Without these, people are simply not productive. In most cases the planners and policy makers are not able to coordinate the recommended programmes, and hence they remain badly uncoordinated at the time of implementation, and so Africa still witnesses the migration of people from rural to urban areas in search of employment. Industries are still being concentrated in towns where better facilities exist, and most African rural areas are still unaffected.

Population policy

Most African countries realize the effect that a high population growth rate may have on economic development. Furthermore, the problem of unemployment is often attributed to the high population growth rate in Africa. It is also argued that the pressure of people on land and capital can reduce the productivity of labour. Therefore programmes have been initiated to combat population problems in Africa, programmes varying a great deal from one country to another.

In some African countries the attitude seems to have been to watch the annual increase with some degree of quiet satisfaction, but in others, attempts have been made to move the population from certain areas to others, and not necessarily to reduce the rate of population growth. Programmes of a non-demographic nature included, for example, agricultural settlement schemes, the deliberate introduction of industries in rural areas, or the industrialization of rural-based crafts. Only a few countries in Africa have come up with clearly stated measures about population and programmes, such as family planning, which have been embarked upon with full governmental support. Nevertheless, population rates continue to rise even in those countries where the governments officially support the programmes, and Kenya is a good example where family planning services have existed since 1965 but the population continues to flourish at a very high rate.

The problems that face these programmes are numerous, the most obvious being that most of them are concentrated in the urban areas leaving a large proportion of the rural population untouched. In most cases, family planning methods have not been free and have had to be paid for; this eliminates their use by individuals from the low-income brackets. Besides, in most African countries the services are still provided by voluntary bodies which often have limited resources. Family planning services have been associated with health services and are not considered a family welfare service. The public can easily confuse it with a medical problem and readily associate it with all sorts of diseases.

In conclusion, most African governments appear to be generally interested in certain population issues, but do not seem to have recognized the need for designing population policies to deal with selected demographic issues. The institutions or programmes established to tackle population problems tend to remain formal legislative or administrative units.

Special groups

In discussing family policy in Africa it is necessary to give special attention to children, youth, the aged, women and refugees. These groups pose unique problems to policy makers and are often overlooked.

Children

In Africa children have been and are still valued both by their parents and society. Most countries have legal systems safe-guarding the rights of children. States make attempts to provide education and health services for the children, although looking after them remains a family affair. This makes the parents see children as property, and especially men see themselves as the owners of the children. This arrangement is only fair for the children if the parents are responsible; and it becomes a problem when the parents fail to play their roles. In such situations the enforcement of the law becomes impossible.

Children also experience great differences in their living conditions, depending on whether the parents are rich or poor. The poor children, both in rural and urban areas, experience difficulties in growing up irrespective of the policies the government may have. In urban areas, they often live in congested conditions with no privacy whatsoever. Often they are exposed to abuse and are introduced to drinking and drug abuse at tender ages. Sometimes parents, in attempts to improve their economic status, encourage them to engage in criminal activities like stealing and house-breaking. At times, in order to get 'free education', as the parents call it, they are advised to get involved in criminal activities in order to go to approved schools, which are confused with free education. In short, most children from low-income groups find difficulty in meeting their needs, and the programmes provided for children in general barely reach them. For example, where there is free primary education, children from poor families may miss their education because they cannot afford uniforms or building funds.

Special groups of children are sometimes not well covered by national policies. These include illegitimate and handicapped children. Most African states tend to be ambivalent about the status of the former, while for many years it has not been considered good economics to support the latter and attitudes are only now starting to change. Children who are orphans are expected to be looked after by the kinsmen, and little regard is taken of the fact that the extended family system is rapidly changing and alternatives have to be found.

The type of education provided for children at primary level leaves poor rural and urban children with more problems than solutions. Primary education tends to prepare the children for secondary education. Most schools in the rural areas and those attended by children from poor families in the towns are often ill-equipped in everything. The majority of children attending these schools find themselves ending their education after primary school. Often they are young and ill-equipped for any job. This leads to unemployment and all forms of frustration for the children, a common factor in most African states.

Youth

Most states have programmes for this group since a large proportion of the African population is made up of young people. There is great variation from one country to another in techniques used to involve youth in national development. Sometimes states have made deliberate efforts to work out appealing programmes to induce young people to participate in national activities, while in others they have left parents and schools to take care of them, whereupon the state blames them for their laxity. Because employment in modern sectors or enterprises does not increase rapidly enough to absorb all school leavers, young people fall victim to this situation, and most of them move from one town to another looking for jobs. It seems that in Africa the young tend to be over-represented among the groups seeking employment and education in urban areas. Failing to realize or to secure their intentions, some remain on the streets and are caught up in law-breaking activities.

In traditional societies, young persons were helped to pass from youth to adulthood, and most were initiated into adult roles and prepared for future responsibilities with minimum conflict. At the moment it seems that African youth has been left to its own resources, and one only needs to visit African cities to witness their lack of direction and unruliness. The programmes provided for them in urban areas are not only expensive, as they are few, but are also sometimes too Western in approach and go counter to the conditions prevailing in some African states. These programmes are often not available in the rural areas, where many young people are idle and sometimes migrate to the urban areas to look for a better life.

The aged

In traditional Africa, old people have been looked after by their children or members of the extended family. They had an important role to play, especially in the education of young people. With changes in Africa, young people now leave the aged in rural communities to come to urban areas and look for jobs, and the old often find themselves being left alone in their rural homes with nobody to attend to them. This creates many problems for the aged, especially in terms of their health needs.

In most countries in Africa, the care of the elderly has been left to their families and only the voluntary bodies have taken on the responsibility of establishing institutions for them. Such homes are not only too few to cater for the elderly population in different African countries, but they are also too alien. Perhaps the idea of building homes for the aged would have been avoided if there were clear policies relating to old age. The lack of deliberate interest or concern for them can be illustrated by the fact that, although 1982 was the International Year of the Aged, few activities were heard of in Africa, compared to the International Years of the women and children.

Women

Because of social and economic change, the African family has been experiencing some change in life styles, and quite a number of women have taken up employment in urban areas for various reasons. In some African countries, such as Ghana, women so far have gained reasonably high positions in society, and engage in employment either to buy themselves whatever they want or to support their families. In other countries, however, such as Kenya, women have taken to work either to support themselves and their families or to subsidize the family income. Whatever the reasons, the traditional ideology about the division of labour still lingers on, and women are still expected to play the roles of wife, mother, homemaker and office worker. This results in a pattern where the activities of the modern African man are actually concentrated outside home. This arrangement does not allow for the need, where both men and women work, for roles also to change.

Most working women do so for long and exhausting hours. They must adopt the usual regular hours of work, and have to leave their homes very early in the morning and return very late in the evening. In most cases there is no institutional care for their infants, and the few pre-schools are quite expensive. This makes the mothers rely on a cheap but an extremely risky type of child care, and in so doing some mothers have lost their babies because they were left with maids who were either too young and inexperienced or others, equally dangerous, with personality problems. All these conditions create major problems for working mothers, and most states tend to overlook them in their policies.

Most working women are not represented through bargaining mechanisms in most African states, and their working conditions remain uncontrolled. This has led to the development of voluntary organizations, run mostly by the same women, to look into women's problems. For example, organizations such as business and professional women's associations are now being established in some African states. Likewise, associations for single mothers or parents are being set up mainly to look into the problems of women for whom state programmes have failed to provide. The most interesting observation is that, although women's organizations are mushrooming in Africa, the same is not true for men. One wonders why African states should allow African women to import foreign ideologies to handle their problems instead of working out measures which could benefit both men and women, thereby strengthening the quality of family life. Another problem of these imported ideologies or programmes is that they tend to address themselves to special groups who claim to be the advocates for the disadvantaged. Often the majority of women, who do not fit in these categories, are left out and suffer in silence.

Refugees

Africa, as other developing regions, is known for its political instability. As a result, Africa has broken records in relation to refugees from both political and economic hardships. So far there has been no deliberate effort to accept the fact that refugees are a problem on the continent and that therefore there is a need to work out explicit policies regarding them. In Africa it is even hard to differentiate between those who are really refugees because of political conditions and those who have decided to live in other countries perhaps because of better facilities in those countries. The lack of policy creates many problems for those individuals who, because of their political convictions, have nowhere to go and live a decent life. Often when a country experiences some internal crisis, refugees from elsewhere are called upon to declare their status; that country realizes the implications of having foreigners sharing their meagre resources – a common phenomenon in Africa at a time of crisis. Such actions are taken without realizing the hardships this particular approach may create for stateless families. Thus, most refugees in Africa tend to live in constant fear, a state that has driven some of them to malpractices and abuse of alcohol. There is nothing so demaning as to be plagued regularly with notices requiring one to report to immigration offices for permits and clarification of status whenever there is some minor internal disturbance. Since Africa is changing so fast, there is no guarantee that there will be no problems that may render persons stateless, and it is vital that clear policies are worked out regarding refugees.

The consequences of family policy

From what has been discussed in this chapter it can be seen that for the most part family policy tends to be implicitly expressed in Africa, and that the meaures that have been taken are really socio-economic policy measures, which are aimed at improving the welfare of the people. Many measures have been introduced, but still more different methods are needed in most countries, with more emphasis being put on the rural rather than urban areas in policy statements. Action will have to be taken, therefore, towards the provision of improved farming techniques, irrigation schemes, credit schemes, small business programmes, community development programmes, cooperative movements, the establishment of rural industries through industrial estates, and settlement schemes.

In some African countries some of the above measures have not been implemented, mainly for economic reasons, but other countries have made genuine efforts to implement them. Where they have been implemented and people have realized large increases in income, other problems have been created. Those incomes, in fact, have not been utilized to improve families' living standards. The irrigation and sugar schemes, for example, have failed to improve the welfare of the farmers. Whenever the farmers get their money after harvest, they tend to misuse the income on drink and excessive use of alcohol has increased in these areas. The family members remain poor while the head of the family – that is, the man – either abuses alcohol or marries more wives.

The education policies have also not benefited families. For example, the provision of free primary education has only benefited those who can afford building funds and uniforms. In poor families the children have to enter the labour market while very young, a situation that has led to child labour in Africa. The type of education offered seems to be irrelevant as soon as it is introduced: for example, technical education has not been useful to most children since the market for the skills acquired has not been growing at a similar pace. This also applies to commercial education, since business has not been developed at the same rate as the demand, and supply and demand has always been incompatible, a situation that has led to unemployment in Africa.

The population measures taken have achieved very little, and the population growth rate remains very high. This is an area that has created problems for women especially – problems not only of using some of the family planning methods, but also of bearing accusations of infidelity by husbands who remain suspicious of family planning.

Although most women, especially those residing in the urban areas, can now work in offices and earn independent incomes, in so doing more problems have been created for them. They still have to run their homes themselves or depend on young and inexperienced house helpers who at times abuse their children in their absence. The mental torture these women experience is tremendous, and at times threatens the stability of their marriage.

With all the legal measures that have been introduced, the African woman has learned that her status has not changed much. If she is married, the husband can still marry other wives and even throw her out of her matrimonial home if he so wishes. If she is unmarried, her illegitimate child may not be supported by the putative father because in certain situations the Affiliation Acts have been repealed. She may not even get a loan from the bank to buy property without her husband's consent.

Family policy measures have, however, also yielded positive results in that states and different groups in society nowadays tend to pay attention to family problems. In addition, much research is being carried out by individuals and institutions on all aspects of the family. It is hoped that this research will in the future throw light upon problems affecting families and that the findings may be used as planning tools for the planners.

6   Theoretical considerations

We may all react more emotionally to theories of the family than to theories in other substantive areas. This is to be expected, since the family is something with which most of us have had very intimate experience. In a way, we have all formulated our own 'theories' about the family based on these personal experiences and our cultural socialization into a particular culture. An example of this comes from a recent lecture on wife-beating. Students had been told that wife-beating may result from the husband's feelings of frustration. The reaction to this explanation was quick and forceful. Students felt that men beat their wives to show their power, not because they were frustrated in any way. They had their own explanation, based upon what they had seen and been told.

It takes a while for new students to understand the utility of theories, especially when what they themselves have seen is contradicted by these theories. If one understands that any theory is simply one person's way of reasoning out what he has seen and from that making general statements, the usefulness of theory should be more obvious. We should see theories as tools to aid us in further observations and research; knowing what is already known helps us to move more quickly into unexplored areas. Since theories are also attempts to explain our observations or our data, new observations which do not 'fit' any theory help us in generating new theoretical perspectives.

Unfortunately, in Third World countries there is a disadvantage in studying the sociology of the family which centres on the relevance of theoretical perspectives developed in very different social contexts. Generally, students have two typical responses. They either reject all theories which were developed elsewhere as irrelevant, or they accept all these theories without questioning their relevance. Certainly, we need a middle road, so that we can critically assess what can safely be used or what we can discard.

Students who read this book are reminded that there is not one theory about the family which is superior to the others or which explains more than others. In fact, we have called this chapter, Theoretical considerations because there are as yet few true theories about the family.

It is hoped that students will discover something about a few theoretical approaches so that they may be better able to:

1) understand their own experiences with families;
2) compare and evaluate these approaches relative to one another; and
3) think about new approaches to replace previous ones that appear inadequate.

Finally, the different approaches usually involve quite different types of data collection, the methods ranging from interviewing and participant observation to case histories. One example should clarify why the matching of theory and methods is vital. If we want to study family conflict, it is not likely that observation alone will tell us much. Asking questions might be possible, although people may not want to admit that there is conflict in their family. What may turn out to be a partial solution is a large number of meetings with selected members of the family, wherein the family members begin to build up confidence in the researcher. Over time, more and more will be revealed about conflict. If the researcher had hoped to observe conflict between husband and wife he would have failed in cultures where such conflict occurs only in private.

Theorizing about the family

In the simplest terms, theories are comprised of concepts or variables which are linked together in propositions. We can say that 'the child's role in the family division of labour affects his performance in school'. Here 'role' and 'performance' are two concepts which are linked together in a simple proposition. Theories link together many such propositions and attempt to explain *why* there is a relationship: *how* does the role affect performance or *why* does poverty lead to drunkenness in one family and not in others?

It has been found, for instance, that higher levels of education usually lead to a reduction in fertility, but we are not totally certain why this should be so. Do higher levels of education change one's outlook about children, or does education give one new ambitions which conflict with the existence of a large family, or does education put one into touch with new reference groups which do not look favourably on large families? When education is found to have a curvilinear relationship with the numbers of children one has, so that the uneducated and the most educated have the largest families, how is this explained? The point is, we must know what it is about education that causes a change in fertility, or what other factors besides education may be causing the change in fertility before we can say we have explained the relationship. Furthermore, the relationships which are shown to be true in one cultural or societal environment must be tested cross-culturally before they can be used to build general theories. As we move from nation to nation, or ethnic group to ethnic group, or class to class, we learn more about specific conditions under which our propositions hold true. We thus begin to develop more sophisticated propositions that incorporate more factors or variables, so that eventually our theory applies throughout the world.

In general, theories are developed through two basic approaches:

1) from observations to theory; or
2) from theory to testing through observations.

The first, or inductive, approach is based on the idea that we should first collect details on human behaviour or attitudes by observing, asking questions or studying existing records. We then make propositions which follow from what we have seen or learned in selected settings. The second, or deductive, approach starts from existing propositions or hypotheses, which may or may not be based on research or empirical data. It proceeds to test these hypotheses in different settings to see whether or not the hypotheses have any generalizability. In the area of African family studies we are more likely to see more of the first approach in the coming years, as indigenous scholars attempt to derive propositions which have African social systems as the substantive base. This should, of course, be linked with general sociological frameworks developed from other situational and national contexts. However, these frameworks would take a somewhat secondary place in African scholastic endeavours so that these frameworks would not, either

1) force researchers to focus on research problems which are of minor importance to African family functioning; or
2) blind the researcher to the uniqueness of African families.

Oversimplifying a complex area like theory any more than we are doing would render a disservice to the reader. Thus, we suggest that students examine a number of works to aid their understanding of processes of theory construction. The most complete book is in two volumes, and is entitled *Contemporary Theories about the Family* (1979). The first volume deals with what are called research-based theories, totals some 668 pages and is edited by Wesley Burr, Reuben Hill, F. Ivan Nye and Iva Reiss who are acknowledged leaders in the field of family sociology in the United States. The second volume deals with general theories such as social exchange, symbolic interaction and a general systems approach to the family. These two volumes could be used for research on the African family in the deductive manner discussed above. Recognizing, of course, that the first volume is based on a deductive model, we are simply noting that the *use* of the two volumes in African contexts would be a deductive approach.

From the viewpoint of working from existing data to formulate propositions based on the African experience, we propose another set of works be used. This set is the Changing African Family Project Series, originating from the Australian National University (Caldwell, 1977; Oppong, 1978; Ware, 1981). The project began in 1972 as a collaborative venture between the Department of Sociology, University of Ibadan, Nigeria, and the Department of Demography, Australian National University. There have been many detailed country studies throughout the continent emerging from this project. The only minor limitation of the series is that the focus is a demographic one, though it is not a rigidly demographic approach. The studies are richly endowed with details about changing family life, as the project intended.

Finally, there are research reports published by the United Nations Economic Commission for Africa on women in Africa. Though focusing on women, the subjects are vital to an understanding of African family life. There are also numerous studies available in national journals that are probably available through inter-library loans. The interchange of research materials among African nationals is not yet well systematized, so that it is often easier for an East African to read an American or British journal than it is to read a West African journal.

We will now be more specific by suggesting how we might work from the inductive or deductive approaches to understand African family life. The deductive approach is covered under the heading 'General approaches to understanding African family life'; and the inductive approach under the heading 'Illustrative models of family phenomena'.

General approaches to understanding African family life

We have chosen to describe the following theoretical approaches in greater detail: Winch's model of family organization, the conflict perspective, and symbolic interactionism. Each could be used as a framework from which to begin analysing the African family.

Winch's (1979) model of family organization is perhaps the most advanced among models that attempt to explain the overall structure of the family. For him, family organization, being the pattern of residence and the size of the family, is determined by the mode of subsistence. The mode of subsistence includes the level of technology, and varies from hunting and fishing, to irrigation agricultural societies. This mode of subsistence is affected by the environmental potentialities such as the extent of population pressure and the ecological setting.

The mode of production does not directly influence family organization, but influences other factors which in turn affect family organization. Thus the mode of production is the most basic though not the only factor contributing to the nature of family organization.

After the mode of subsistence, the factors of 'surplus and social relations of production' and the 'nature of work' are important. These two terms generally encompass much of what is included in Marx and Engels' theoretical work. Engels looked at industrialization as the underlying condition for the emergence of small families which were 'functional' to the capitalist system of production. Numerous authors, such as Etienne and Leacock (1980) and Gough (1961), see the spread of the unitary market system as the root cause of kinship change. By the nature of work, Winch means the division of labour in the family.

At the next level, Winch argues that socialization, social inequality, settlement type, system of inheritance and residence patterns all enter into the relationship. They are the remaining five factors which determine familial organization. The model then begins from the mode of production and ends with these five factors.

The model is intended to explain differences in family organization but not the internal processes or functioning of the family. We could use the model to understand why in some ways African families are so different from Western families. Whereas in Western societies many people work in industries and live in towns, in African societies the people are primarily involved in agriculture. It could then be argued that differences in family organization are merely reflections of the mode of production (MacGaffey, 1983:187). Internal to African societies one could conceivably compare the families of pastoral farmers, rural large-scale farmers and urban dwellers on the basis of Winch's model.

Winch's model is largely a deterministic one in the way that the family organization is seen as determined or caused by all the other factors rather than the family organization also causing changes in any of these other factors. Koenig's (1981) work, mentioned in the last section, shows somewhat different results from those that Winch predicted. The family groups studied by Koenig selected cash crops which suited their family or traditional organization rather than altering their family organization to fit ecological and cropping variabilities. We are also aware that a general model like Winch's is useful for comparing families in very diverse economic systems such as the communist and capitalist systems. Thus we cannot easily dismiss his model without running the risk of ignoring the major role of these economic systems.

He does focus solely on the structure of families and, as he points out, his analysis is limited to the type of ethnographic data which are available. We prefer not to evaluate Winch's or any of the following two approaches but simply to summarize the essence of these approaches. The next two approaches deal with the internal functioning rather than the structure of the family.

The conflict perspective is the next approach to be reviewed. Sprey (1979) applied a general conflict approach to the study of the family. He begins with a list of assumptions underlying this approach. For example, one assumption is that human beings enter most relationships as real or potential competitors. Another assumption is that there is a perpetual scarcity of resources in the society and, we could often say, also within the family. There are societal inequalities which result in unequal allocation of these scarce resources.

One of the basic concepts of the conflict approach is competition, which is a relationship wherein one person gains at the expense of another's loss. Conflict is a second basic concept. Conflict refers to a confrontation between two or more people or dyads or groups over scarce resources, or goals or means to achieve goals (Sprey, 1979:134). Conflict may involve negotiation, power, aggression or threats. Conflict can vary from physical force to less violent strategies like litigation.

Finally, there are processes which deal with the end of conflict. Conflict resolution and management have both been used. Conflict resolution implies that competition or conflict of interest among family members is totally eliminated. However, elimination of competition or conflict of interest is usually impossible and undesirable in some respects. It is now thought to be unhealthy for individuals to pretend that they are happy with a family situation when they are not. Klein's (1975) book, *The Myth of the Happy Child*, says that parents often discourage their children from expressing their feelings so that when the child is silent or quiet the parent believes that this is a measure of happiness, but this happiness is a myth. 'Conflict management' is a preferable term to 'conflict resolution'. 'Management' implies that competition still exists but in a manageable form. Family members can learn to manage their differences without pretending there are none.

The conflict perspective is suggested here for a variety of reasons. We began this book by highlighting the complexity and variety of social changes that have taken place or are taking place in Africa. Changes that took place over centuries elsewhere are happening in a matter of decades. It is obvious that conflict not order should be a common phenomenon in family living in this situation.

Traditional systems of marriage exist simultaneously with modern civil systems. As we noted, there are conflicts in marriage generated by the discrepancy between these two systems. Legally, the cases are mounting; they deal with inheritance, rights over children, divorce and conflict between rules of distinctive systems in cases of inter-ethnic marriage.

Opportunities for advancement are seldom similar for all family members. While one son may attain a Ph.D., another never attends school. One brother becomes a rich businessman and the other a poor peasant farmer. One child inherits land while the others go to squat in the city. The underlying tension is created not by unequal opportunities alone but by the African family ethic of reciprocity. Those who advance must help those who have not risen so far.

The means to achieve family goals could also be fruitfully examined in the light of a conflict model. Role allocation is a means of attaining the family's goals of socialization and upbringing of children. When there are serious inequalities in role allocation between members of the household, conflict often involves wife-beating, fighting among children or depression of members, especially the woman. Development programmes may exacerbate existing family role conflicts by favouring one sex over the other.

The spread of some religious groups has meant that all of what would be open conflict is submerged through a number of techniques such as being 'saved', or being possessed or submitting to one's husband (regardless of his character, personality or behaviour). Yet this submerging of conflict is nothing new to Africa, because in many systems open conflict among family members was avoided. Verbal arguments between husband and wife were rare, and non-existent between parents and children. Serious disagreements between the mother-in-law and the daughter-in-law were likely to be resolved by sending the daughter-in-law away rather than letting the two settle their differences openly. Conflicts were also managed through witchcraft rather than direct confrontation.

In general, the conflict approach would be suitable. The conflicts are many, but also the nature and management of conflict is very different from what occurs in other societies.

Finally, we look at symbolic interactionism. Symbolic interactionism is based on the assumption that symbols are important in understanding human behaviour. Symbols are words or ideas that have meaning. They are derived from interaction with others. Furthermore, the approach assumes that the human actor is a reactor who can influence phenomena as well as being influenced. In symbolic interactionism, terms such as the 'self', 'reference groups', 'roles' and 'organismic involvement' are used. Examples of organismic involvement, given by Burr (1979) and his co-authors, are being the object of sorcery or witchcraft and hysteria.

Role theory is well developed, having a number of aspects. There is the notion of the quality of role enactment referring to the extent to which a person fulfils normative role expectations. In a marital relationship, the husband or mother-in-law may be the one who decides on the quality of role enactment by the wife, although the wife is not allowed to assess similarly the quality of role performance of the husband or mother-in-law.

There may be consensus on role expectations, so that the husband and wife both clearly agree on what they expect the other to do in the family. However, it often happens that there is little consensus on what the role expectations are for each individual. The mother may be expected by her husband to cook, to help children with their homework and manage a full-time job, yet she places importance only on the last two roles. Thus, lack of consensus exists, and conflicts or unhappiness are likely to result.

Symbolic interactionism also helps us deal with the notion of transition into roles. The traditional initiation ceremonies had a wealth of symbolic meaning that is lost once the physical operation is conducted in hospitals. Many other societies suffer from problems stemming from lack of clear transitions into roles. Perhaps the traditional ceremonies suggest avenues for easing the transition into roles in modern Africa.

There have also been innovative studies of social class and socialization using symbolic interactionism as a framework. Class has symbolic dimensions which are missed in the typical classification of individuals according to objective social groupings. Family members may feel relatively deprived if their reference group members are more successful. Children also learn from an early age if they are disadvantaged compared to others, and may react by withdrawing or fearing interaction with better-off children. Some families prepare the children better for such environments like schools through the particular style of language and thought processes used in the home. Work by Bernstein focuses on this subject.

Family communication processes are better understood in terms of symbolic interactionism than most other perspectives. Family members have gestures that are commonly used. Some families use gestures more than words to communicate, or spatial distance more than words. Communication in African families may de-emphasize mutual decision-making in preference to such gestures and spatial distinctions.

In summary, symbolic interactionism would provide another useful theoretical framework with which to study African families. Symbolic aspects of African life involve such aspects as use of witchcraft in conflict, and the relationship of certain ceremonies with the world of the ancestors. Interpretation of misfortunes like death, sickness and insanity are best analysed with symbolic interactionism. Reference groups are even more important as class differences increase and families aspire to upward mobility for their children. Role performance and the hidden meaning in family communication are both amenable to analysis by symbolic interactionism.

Illustrative models of family phenomena

As well as using more general theoretical approaches we may theorize about the family by using models, which are diagrammatic representations of all the factors we believe are causally related to an object of our interest. We base such a model on research work on African families or on what we ourselves have observed to happen in African families. We begin by listing the variables or factors we feel are important, and then draw a diagram containing all the variables. The purpose is to understand the African family better, systematizing what we know in diagrammatic form.

Suppose we want to explain the amount and variety of the child's labour contributions in the African family. We would, after a period of reflection, perhaps come up with a model such as that given on page 101. The model tells us that the society, the family, schools and the child's personal characteristics affect the amount of work children do. It was actually derived from research or observation on African families and thus represents a deductive approach.

Let us discuss the model more carefully. The arrows indicate suggested lines of causation. The societal factors influence the child's work through their influence on the family. There are direct causal lines between the child's work and the family, the schools and the child's personal characteristics. These direct lines simply tell us that any of these factors could affect children's work independently without going through or being mediated by other factors.

We begin by trying to explain why any of the lines represents a possible causal relationship. Cultural factors will affect the family in terms of the definition of sex roles and the conception of children. Families which are more traditional would be more susceptible to these cultural influences than the more modern families. Sex roles tell us what a good woman or man, mother or father, son or daughter is in terms of expected behaviour. The culture may condone father's employment outside the home while strongly condemning mother's work outside the house. Young male children are expected to herd, while female children should be helping in mother's duties. There are also conceptions about children and their role in society: children must help their parents in old age; children should do what they are told to do; children are God's gift and should not be overworked or harmed in any way.

National policies would affect the families which are better integrated into society more than marginal families. (Examples of national policies are the legal system and the educational system.) Prohibiting children from working will perhaps lead to parents withdrawing children from wage labour which is illegal, and using the children's labour in the home to replace their own labour while they (the parents) pick up outside work. More importantly, however, would be the educational system, including such features as the number of places, the quality of schools, compulsory attendance rules and support given to both sexes to attend school.

The social environment may also affect the family's practice of using

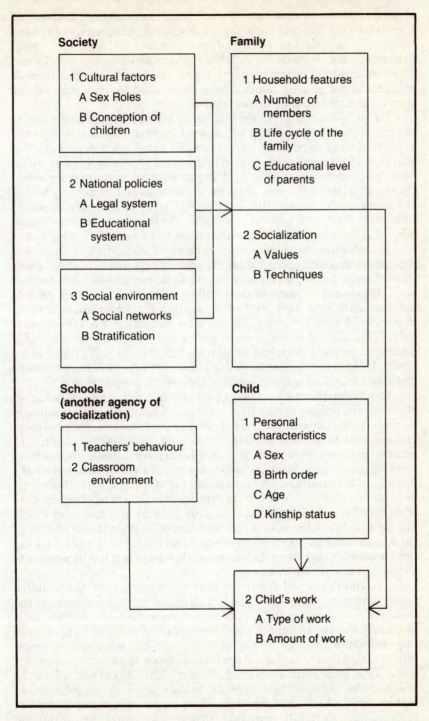

Model of children's work in the family

children's labour in a number of ways. Social networks of relatives and friends may act either to encourage or discourage children's work in the house. These relatives or friends are sources of influence whose behaviour may be modelled or whose advice may be closely followed. The stratification system patterns could also determine the family's practices. Poor peasant families have more need for children's labour than do the middle-class urban families.

At the household level, the number of members in the family means the number of people among whom work can be shared, as well as the amount of work to be done. Larger families entail much more work, but also have more people able to help in this work. A younger family would have fewer members capable of doing an adult's job, so that we would realize that the life cycle may be another causal factor explaining children's work. Finally, the educational level of the parents would influence their attitude to children's work, their feelings about schooling and their conception of the requisites of a child's development.

In addition to household features, socialization values and techniques may be responsible for the amount and quality of child labour in the family. Some parents may believe that responsibility is the major value they want to instil in their children, whereas for other parents independence or a high level of motivation for achievement is more important. There are other parents who emphasize work over other values. On the other hand, some parents use work assignments as a technique to instil discipline or to train the child in skills required by adults. If children are given work as a punishment they will learn to resent work and may find ways of shirking their work assignments.

In schools, the teachers may order children not to help at home or, alternatively, tell them to help their parents. Children may thus willingly do more work at home or refuse to help their parents at all. The classroom environment may be conducive to learning, encouraging children to succeed in their school work. If a child is very enthusiastic about school work he may neglect his home duties not out of stubbornness but simply because of his priorities. The sex ratio in the classroom is another subtle influence on children's work. If children see this ratio to be comparable to what they have experienced in their daily life they may feel comfortable and do well. When the ratio is very imbalanced – say, in favour of males – the female children may feel out of place and concentrate more on doing their household tasks than their homework, feeling that it is impossible to succeed in a male environment.

The child's sex will determine the type of work, with male children doing 'masculine' tasks and female children doing 'feminine' tasks unless there are no children of the opposite sex to do certain jobs. Birth order is also likely to have an impact, since an older child will tend to have more responsibilities than his young siblings. Age has somewhat different effects in that the chronological age relates closely to physical capacity for work. Thus, even a first-born child, if under eight years of age, will not be assigned the same amount of work usually given to an older, more mature child. As a child becomes older he also gains more sense of responsibility so that he may be assigned more dangerous or difficult tasks. Kinship status refers to whether the child was born in or adopted into, or is a distant relative of, the family he lives with.

We have illustrated the construction of a model. It helps to clarify one's thinking about the family. Once the model is drawn, based on research or on what one has observed, one can then look through classical books or textbooks on the family or on general theory to try to explain each line or all the lines of causation together.

Our second model deals with the factors which influence the mother's involvement in wage labour (see page 104). At the societal level, the day-care facilities and services for working mothers would affect the woman's decision about whether working would be detrimental to her children or herself in any way. If there are few or no jobs available, she will have no real opportunity to work.

In the family, the husband's support is the most critical factor. He may order his wife to go out and find work, or he may allow her to work or forbid her from working. While allowing her to work he may discourage her by complaining about her family role performance, or encourage her by helping her complete her work in the house. Relatives and friends may advise a woman to stay home or go to work, or provide contacts for employment. The number of children in the family will determine the extent of financial need, the number of helpers one can count on to help the mother, or the quantity of alternative child-care arrangements that would be involved.

In Africa, the quantity and quality of house workers in the home is more important than the societal child-care facilities. If the woman has a dependable worker, she may readily take up employment. If workers are unreliable, a woman may begin work, but never get into high positions because of frequent absences from work. The family life cycle is relevant here primarily in terms of the number of very young children, the financial status of the family, and the age of the woman.

As for the woman herself, her self-perception will influence her attempts at getting work and her quality of presentation in interviews. Her education level and her job experience will affect her preparedness for work. The career goals will orient her towards certain types of work, and would also influence when she works during the family life cycle.

The final factor, the mother's employment, is first of all concerned with the amount of time in a week that she devotes to outside work. Number of years refers to the total continuous work time or total work time over separate periods in her lifetime.

These two models have illustrated how internal features of the family and societal factors can be related to problems of interest to us. More importantly, they have shown how one may work with the reality of the African family more effectively, by beginning from the reality and deriving a total picture of how the family operates.

The African family: a converging phenomenon?

If one does not read certain works on the family carefully enough, one may too quickly assume that all families in all cultural environments

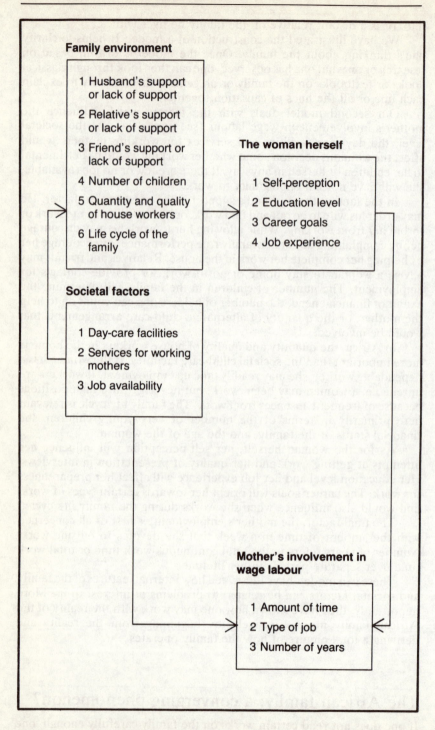

Family environment

1 Husband's support
   or lack of support

2 Relative's support
   or lack of support

3 Friend's support or
   lack of support

4 Number of children

5 Quantity and quality
   of house workers

6 Life cycle of the
   family

The woman herself

1 Self-perception

2 Education level

3 Career goals

4 Job experience

Societal factors

1 Day-care facilities

2 Services for working
   mothers

3 Job availability

**Mother's involvement in
wage labour**

1 Amount of time

2 Type of job

3 Number of years

Model of mother's involvement in wage labour

change towards a similar type of family due to forces of modernization, urbanization and industrialization. Reputable theorists such as Goode (1963) have argued that there is indeed a convergence towards a conjugal family in which:

1) the extended family is rare;
2) there is free choice of spouse;
3) the authority of the parent over the child and of the husband over the wife declines; and
4) there is equality of sexes, especially in inheritance.

Yet, while not disputing that such changes are in evidence in Africa, we do object to the idea that these characteristics alone are sufficient to describe fully an African family. Furthermore, to say that the characteristics are more common does not permit us to conclude that the African family is changing from one form to another.

Laslett (1972) in his introduction to *Household and Family in Past Time* indicates that much of the claim for the universality of the nuclear family (another term similar to the 'conjugal family') was based on models of what people believed existed rather than on substantive historical documentation of differences in household and family form. Vaughan (1983) deals with methodological problems of studying the history of the family in Africa. Historical research on the family has in fact become popular only in America and Europe in the last two decades, so we still have much work to be done.

Nevertheless, we can make some general concluding statements about the possibility of African families converging towards any one model on the basis of studies already completed. We noted in Chapter 1, in the section headed 'Characteristics of African family life', that despite changes certain features, like the importance of children to the family and kin group, have endured. These enduring features make it difficult to equate African family life with Western models of family life, especially Goode's conjugal family as described above. More specifically, however, we feel that convergence is unlikely in the near future for the following reasons.

First of all, particular traditional values of family life are not only being retained but are actually being integrated with modern family characteristics with a resulting synthesis of diverse systems of family life into a new socio-cultural model. Thus, African family life is neither purely traditional nor purely Western.

Christian marriages are still often accompanied by payment of bridewealth to the wife's parents, even though bridewealth was initially opposed by the churches. The immediate family and other relatives may delay the church ceremony for hours, refusing to hand the bride over to the groom, until a higher bridewealth is promised. Other couples agree to live together without a formal ceremony, yet when arguments occur, the woman will remind the man that he has not paid her parents anything, referring to bridewealth, and thus indicating that he has little authority over her. He may also never treat this woman as his wife since he has not paid bridewealth, and may eventually leave her and marry another woman for whom bridewealth is paid.

Some well-educated African husbands and wives may adopt the leisure patterns of Western families, such as going out together very often and spending holidays together, yet each may have an individual bank account and operate with separate budgets for household expenditures. Husbands and wives also spend more time in discussions about disciplining children, treatment of extended kin-group members and about their lifetime goals, but when there is a disagreement with the wife the husband may still act in an authoritarian manner.

There is also a great deal of integration of the traditional African religious–cultural beliefs and practices, together with more modern practices, even among the educated. When a woman gives birth to a deformed child, a husband who knows the possible genetic causes of this deformation may still strongly believe that the problem was caused by unfaithfulness by the wife. In other instances, a husband or wife with a fertility problem may go for traditional cures that may be only partly medical or based on herbal treatment. Infertility cures often involve much psychological treatment. Temporary insanity of the wife may respond well to traditional cures, but may not be helped at all by modern psychiatric care. If a wife tries to commit suicide, very often because of pressures from her husband's relatives living with her, the husband may easily blame her attempted suicide on someone bewitching her. Thus, traditional beliefs and practices continue to be an integral part of much of family life.

Studies of family size illustrate how resilient some values can be, even when social scientists assumed that such values had been totally eliminated. Family size, in terms of numbers of children, declined over time, with social scientists hastening to argue that a downward linear trend was the direction of change in the future. After stabilization of economic resources and increased economic security, family size went up again. Husbands are also very much against family planning techniques which are rather permanent, such as tubal ligation, even after the wife has given birth to four or five children. Any wife who has this operation done without her husband's consent may be divorced according to laws in many African nations. Finally, the reluctance to adopt children legally shows that adopted children *per se* are not an acceptable substitute for childless young couples. Instead, the husband will usually marry another wife in preference to adopting.

Polygyny and the Islamic rule of seclusion of women are other values that have persisted after a period of decline. Polygyny seems initially to increase in urban areas and then decline with the level of economic development. There are as well strong indications that the decline in official polygyny may have been replaced by an unofficial polygyny in the keeping of 'mistresses'. Seclusion of Moslem married women has become more commonly practised in places where prosperity has increased.

Another reason why convergence of the family is unlikely in the near future is the high degree of cultural diversity on the continent. There is little chance that all the diverse cultural groups on the continent would adopt one family form and life style – therefore much less chance of all groups converging towards a conjugal family type. Let us consider what this cultural diversity means. In the first place, it means that the beginning point – that is, the traditional African family – is not a uniform, homogeneous type for all cultural groups. There are cases where the 'traditional' African form has many of the so-called Western characteristics. Koenig's (1981) research among the Basa (of southern Cameroon) and the Manding (of Mali) is a recent illustration of this point. The Basa prefer smaller families and have a low degree of inter-familial reciprocity, while the Manding prefer larger families and strong extended family ties. Koenig says that each group adopted cash crops which suited the ecology and the traditional social organization, with the result that very few changes in family life or structure occurred over time. Thus, the changes over time have not always been from the stereotyped features of African life to the Western ones. Some Western features have been common for specific ethnic groups for many decades.

Secondly, cultural diversity means that the direction, magnitude and type of family change may vary drastically from one group to the next so that again it becomes hard to conceptualize an ideal type of African family. Rather, we can only justifiably speak of common characteristics but not of an ideal type in the sense it is used in the process of theorizing in sociology.

Nelson (1978–1979) notes that studies have shown a decrease in polygyny, bridewealth and the lineage-clan systems for the Kikuyu although the opposite is true for the Luo, another group within Kenya. Hence change affects groups differently so that their characteristics may be culturally more distinct over time rather than more similar to other groups.

One of the more important reasons why convergence seems so far off is the role of the extended family. Sennett's (1970) work is the most recent and systematic exploration of the essential role of the extended family in facilitating instead of hindering the success of the nuclear family unit in the urban environment. Since the urban environment is often only one part of a complex set of changes in the economy, in educational systems and in personal relationships, we can say that the extended family could as well have a positive role in linking families with the national development process both in rural and urban areas. However, this is contrary to the implication fostered by the work on the family of Talcott Parsons and his associates that the nuclear family is most suited to modern occupational and economic systems.

Perhaps the issue is one of emphasis on special or fortunate individuals from any one nuclear family rather than on the success of all the members of a nuclear family. If we are concerned with an entire nuclear family advancing, Sennett's work shows that the nuclear family which maintains strong extended kin relationships is more upwardly mobile than the nuclear family which isolates itself from extended family relationships.

In Africa, the extended family is responsible for a lot of strain but we should then be even more cautious about arguing that the strains signal the death of the extended family system or that the elimination of extended family ties is the best thing that could happen to the African family. So, while accepting the negative aspects of extended families, we must as well acknowledge the benefits. These benefits partially explain the resilience of the extended family throughout periods of colonial oppression, revolutionary struggles and economic strains of national development.

On the continent, the African extended family still determines many types of ritual obligations and 'African civilized behaviour'. To the African, it is uncivilized to abandon old people to their own resources, or totally to neglect a poor relative's child or to ignore the widow. Even if constant demands from kin-group members eventually lead to some hostility towards relatives, most people still feel obliged to give a great deal of assistance to kin-group members. The only difference between current practice and recent historical patterns is that now people feel more able to reject some demands and select relatives who they feel are more worthy of receiving help.

In other cases, the extended family starts business enterprises which assist the less wealthy to compete in very advanced economic systems. Self-help groups, which try to improve the economic and social welfare of members, often begin as kin-based groups before incorporating non-kin members. People frequently obtain jobs through intervention of kin members, even after obtaining degrees that should have enabled them easily to qualify for existing jobs.

Young children are still sent to live with relatives for schooling and for other reasons. Young adults join urban relatives to look for work. Once these young people obtain work they repatriate large portions of their income to the less fortunate relatives in rural areas even after they have started their own families. University students use part of their scholarships or loan money to help in paying school fees for brothers, sisters or cousins.

The point of all these examples is that the African extended family in terms of its various functions is not rare. What may be rare is the physical contiguity of extended family members, and yet lack of physical contiguity is more a result of housing constraints than of personal preferences.

The next reason why congruence is unlikely is the lack of practical egalitarianism. In other words, when egalitarianism exists in a few spheres of activity but not in others, egalitarianism becomes impractical since most individuals operate in many spheres. Freedom of action and ability to influence others are easily curtailed by the fact that there are many spheres of activity where women are still subordinate to men. Educational opportunities have made women more equal to men and children more equal to parents. Expansion of occupational opportunities have provided women with better incomes and perhaps more independent decision-making. Self-help groups have often made women the major family bread winners or income earners. In all these cases, the husbands are slow to grant women equal authority or decision-making power in the house. Many well-educated women act very submissively towards their husbands in front of other people, sometimes as a mark of respect but perhaps because the husband demands such behaviour.

Furthermore, women who are 'equivalent' to men outside the home, are not exempted from traditional home duties, and so become overburdened trying to maintain both a prestigious job and a strenuous,

low-prestige homemaker role. Educational and occupational opportunities also do not result in practical egalitarianism if economic or
property rights are not concomitant with the women's upward mobility in
these other spheres. Changes in inheritance laws or in property status are
very gradually implemented. Even when these laws are implemented,
popular opinion tends to discourage husbands from making wives equal
owners of land, houses or businesses.

Finally, the reality of African conjugal life is far from the common
idea of intimacy in conjugal families. Intimacy between husband and wife
in public, or in front of relatives and their own children is frowned upon.
A private, intimate life for the husband and wife apart from other
relatives is uncommon. Relatives may participate in the most personal
matters. Husbands and wives may seldom spend time alone together in
leisure activities. The husband and wife's personal knowledge of each
other is not emphasized, and the open expression of love is considered as
unnecessary.

Our opinion, based on all these reasons, is that, in general, the
African family represents a synthesis of traditional and Western family
forms. Like Magubane (1971), we do not feel that the mere listing of
characteristics adopted from other cultures, particularly of the former
colonizers, is sufficient to describe change. As he noted, some adoptions
were suited for survival in a colonial environment, and others proved
relevant beyond the colonial period. Yet the African family is undergoing
rapid change, change which is often not fully understandable through
either simple descriptions of African family life or forms or through use of
theories based solely on studies of non-African societies. After more
detailed studies by researchers on some of the issues covered in this
textbook, we may then start postulating on the rationale of conceiving of
one common synthesis of African family life, or, instead, conceptualizing
African variations on a common family form.

References

ADEPOJU, ADERANTI. 'Rationality and fertility in the traditional Yoruba society, Southest Nigeria', in *The Persistence of High Fertility*, J. Caldwelsociety, Southwest Nigeria', in *The Persistence of High Fertility*, J. Caldwell (ed.)

ALDOUS, JOAN. 'Urbanization, the extended family and kinship ties in West Africa', *Social Forces* 41 (1962), 6–12.

ARONOFF, JOEL, and WILLIAM D. CRANO. 'A re-examination of the cross-cultural principles of task segregation and sex role differentiation in the family', *American Sociological Review* 40 (Feb. 1975), 12–20.

ARONOFF, JOEL and WILLIAM D. CRANO. 'Expressive and instrumental role complementarity in the family' *American Sociological Review* 43 (Aug. 1978), 463–70.

AROWOLO, OLADELE. 'Plural marriage, fertility and the problem of multiple causation', in *Women, Education and Modernization of the Family in West Africa*, Helen Ware (ed.) Canberra, Australian National University, 1981, pp. 112–33.

ARYEE, A. F. 'Urbanization and plural marriage', in *Marriage, Fertility and Parenthood in West Africa*, C. Oppong *et al.* (eds) Canberra, Australian National University, 1978, pp. 368–79.

BERNSTEIN, BASIL. *Class, Codes and Control*, Vol. I, London, Routledge & Kegan Paul, 1971.

BROOKS, GEORGE E. 'The *signares* of Saint-Louis and Goree: women entrepreneurs in eighteenth-century Senegal', in *Women in Africa*, Nancy J. Hafkin and Edna G. Bay (eds) Stanford, Cal., Stanford University Press, 1976, pp. 19–44.

BROWN, JUDITH. 'Cross-cultural perspectives on middle-aged women', *Current Anthropology*, 23 (No. 2, 1982), 143–56.

BURR, WESLEY, REUBEN HILL, F. IVAN NYE and IRA REISS (eds), *Contemporary Theories about the Family*, Vols I and II, New York, Free Press, 1979.

BURR, WESLEY, GEOFFREY K. LEIGH, RANDALL DAY and JOHN CONSTANTINE. 'Symbolic interaction and the family', in *Contemporary Theories about the Family* Wesley Burr *et al.* (eds) Vol. II, New York, Free Press, 1979, pp. 42–111.

CALDWELL, JOHN C. (ed.) *The Persistence of High Fertility*, Canberra, Australian National University, No. 1, Part 1, 1977.

CALDWELL, JOHN C. 'Towards a restatement of demographic transition theory' in *The Persistence of High Fertility*, John Caldwell (ed.) Australian National University, 1977, pp. 25–122.

CHAYANOV, A. V. *The Theory of the Peasant Economy*, Daniel Thorner *et al.* (eds), Homewood, Ill., American Economics Association, 1966.

CLARK, MARI. 'Support networks and survival strategies of the urban poor: a review of the Kenyan literature', Urban and Regional Report Nos. 82–89, Urban and Regional Economics Division, The World Bank, 1982.

CLIGNET, REMI. 'Environmental change, types of descent and child-rearing practices', in *The City in Modern Africa,* Horace Miner (ed.), London, The Pall Mall Press, 1967, pp. 215–56.

CLIGNET, REMI. *Many Wives, Many Powers*, Evanston, Ill., Northwestern University Press, 1970.

COHEN, ABNER. *Custom and Politics in Urban Africa*, Berkeley, Cal., University of California, 1969.

COKER, G. B. *Family Property among the Yorubas*, London, Sweet and Maxwell, 1958.

DE LANCEY, VIRGINIA. 'Wage earner and mother: compatibility of roles on a Cameroon plantation', in *Women, Education and Modernization of the Family in West Africa*, Helen Ware (ed.), Canberra, Australian National University, 1981, pp. 1–21.

DUPIRE, MARGUERITE. 'The position of women in pastoral society', in *Women of Tropical Africa,* Denise Paulme (ed.), London, Routledge & Kegan Paul, 1960, pp. 47–92.

ETIENNE, E. M. and ELEANOR LEACOCK (eds), *Women and Colonization*, New York, Praeger, 1980, pp. 186–213.

FANON, FRANTZ. *The Wretched of the Earth*, Grove Press, New York 1963.

FANON, FRANTZ. *Black Skin, White Masks*, Grove Press, New York 1967.

FATHY, HASSAN. *Architecture for the Poor*, Chicago, Chicago University Press, 1973.

GAMBLE, DAVID, P. 'The Temne family in a modern town in Sierra Leone', *Africa* 33 (July 1963), 209–26.

GOODE, WILLIAM J. *World Revolution and Family Patterns*, Glencoe, Ill., Free Press, 1963.

GOODY, ESTHER. 'Delegation of parental roles in West Africa and West Indies', in *Changing Social Structure in Ghana*, Jack Goody (ed.), London, International African Institute, 1975, pp. 137–65.

GOUGH, KATHLEEN. 'The modern disintegration of matrilineal descent groups', in *Matrilineal Kinship*, D. M. Schneider and Kathleen Gough (eds), Berkeley, Cal., University of California, 1961, pp. 631–54.

GRAY, R. F., and P. H. GULLIVER (eds). *The Family Estate in Africa*, London, Routledge & Kegan Paul, 1964.

GUGLER, JOSEF and WILLIAM FLANAGAN. *Urbanization and Social Change in West Africa*, London, Cambridge University Press, 1978.

GULLIVER, P. H. *Social Control in an African Society*, London, Routledge & Kegan Paul, 1963.

HARRELL-BOND, B. E. *Modern Marriage in Sierra Leone*, The Hague, Paris, Mouton, 1975.

HARRELL-BOND, B. E. 'Stereotypes of Western and African patterns of marriage and family life', *Journal of Marriage and the Family*, 38 (May, 1976), 387–96.

HARRELL-BOND, B. E. and U. RIJSDORP. 'The emergence of the "stranger-permit marriage" and other forms of conjugal union in rural Sierra Leone', in *Law and the Family in Africa*, Simon Roberts (ed.), The Hague, Paris, Mouton, 1977, pp. 205–23

HAY, MARGARET, J. 'Luo woman and economic change during the colonial period', in *Women in Africa*, Nancy J. Hafkin and Edna Bay, Stanford, Cal., Stanford University Press, 1976, pp. 87–109.

HERBST, P. 'The measurement of family relationships', *Human Relations 5* (No. 1, 1952), 3–36.

HILL, POLLY. *Rural Hausa: a Village and Setting*, Cambridge, Cambridge University Press, 1972.

HOEK-SMITH, JUDITH, and ANITA SPRING (eds). *Women in Ritual and Symbolic Roles*, New York, Plenum Press, 1978.

HULL, RICHARD. *African Cities and Towns before the European Conquest*, New York, Norton, 1976.

JULES-ROSETTE, BENNETTA. 'Changing aspects of women's initiation in Southern Africa: an exploratory study', *Canadian Journal of African Studies* 13 (No. 3, 1980), 389–406.

KABWEGYERE, TARSIS. 'Determinants of fertility: a discussion of change in the family among the Akamba of Kenya', in *The Persistence of High Fertility*, J. Caldwell (ed.), Canberra, Australian National University, 1977, pp. 189–221.

KARANJA, WAMBUI. 'Women and work', in *Women, Education, and Modernization of the Family in West Africa*, Helen Ware (ed.), Canberra, Australian National University, 1981, pp. 42–66.

KISEMBO, BENEZERI, LAURENTI MAGESA and AYLWARD SHORTER. *African Christian Marriage*, London, Geoffrey Chapman, 1977.

KLEIN, CAROL. *The Myth of the Happy Child*, New York, Harper & Row, 1975.

KNOWLES, JAMES, and RICHARD ANKER. 'An analysis of income transfers in a developing country: the case of Kenya', *Journal of Development Economics* 8 (1981), 205–226.

KOENIG, DOLORES. 'The stable African family', in *Women, Education and Modernization of the Family in West Africa*, Helen Ware (ed.), Canberra, Australian National University, 1981, pp. 88–107.

KONGSTAD, PER, and METTE MONSTED. *Family, Labour and Trade in Western Kenya*, Uppsala, Scandinavian Institute of African Studies, 1980.

KRIGE, EILEEN JENSEN. 'Women-marriage, with special reference to the Lovedu', *Africa* 44 (Jan. 1974) 11–36.

KUMEKPOR, TOM, K. 'Rural women and attitudes to family planning, contraceptive practice and abortion in Southern Ghana', Department of Sociology, University of Ghana, Legon, 1970.

KUPER, HILDA. 'The Swazi of Swaziland', in *Peoples of Africa*, Jack Gibbs (ed.), Holt, Rinehart and Winston, New York, 1965, pp. 481–511.

KURIA, GIBSON, K. 'Trends in marriage and succession laws in Kenya, 1886–1977', Kenya Historical Association Conference paper, Nairobi, 1977.

LANTUM, DAVID. 'Population dynamics of rural Cameroon and its public health repercussions', University of Cameroon, Yaounde, Oct. 1979.

LASLETT, PETER (ed.). *Household and Family in Past Time*, Cambridge, Cambridge University Press, 1972.

LEVINE, ROBERT, NANCY H. KLEIN, and CONSTANCE R. OWEN. 'Father–child relationships and changing life styles in Ibadan, Nigeria', in *The City in Modern Africa*, Horace Miner (ed.), London, The Pall Mall Press, 1967, pp. 215–56.

LEWIS, OSCAR. *Children of Sanchez*, Penguin Books, Harmondsworth, 1961.

MACGAFFEY, WYATT. 'Lineage structure, marriage and the family amongst the central Bantu' *Journal of African History,* 24(2), 1983, 173–88.

MAGUBANE, B. 'A critical look at indices used in the study of social change in colonial Africa', *Current Anthropology* 12 (1971), 419–44.

MAIR, LUCY *African Societies*, London, Cambridge University Press, 1974.

MARRIS, PETER *The Family and Social Change in an African City*, London, Routledge & Kegan Paul, 1966.

MARRIS, PETER, and ANTHONY SOMERSETT *African Businessmen*, Nairobi, East African Publishing House, 1971.

MARSHALL, GLORIA 'Women, trade and the Yoruba family', unpublished Ph.D. thesis, New York, Columbia University, 1964.

MARSHALL, LORNA. 'The !Kung of the Kalahari Desert', in *Peoples of Africa*, Jack Gibbs (ed.), New York, Holt, Rinehart and Winston, 1965, pp. 241–78.

MBILINYI, MARJORIE. 'The new woman and traditional norms in Tanzania', *Journal of Modern African Studies*, 10 (1972), 57–72.

MBITI, JOHN S. *African Religions and Philosophy*, London, Heinemann, 1969.

MICHAELWAIT, D. R. *Women in rural development*, Boulder, Colorado, Westview Press, 1976.

MINER, HORACE. *The Primitive City of Timbuctoo*, Princeton, N. J., Princeton University Press, 1953.

MURRAY, COLIN. *Families Divided*, Johannesburg, Oxford University Press, 1981.

MUELLER, MARTHA. 'Women, and men, power and powerlessness in Lesotho', in *Women and National Development*, Wellesley Editorial Committee (ed.), Chicago, University of Chicago Press, 1977, pp. 154–66.

NELSON, NICCI. 'Female-centred families: changing patterns of marriage and family among buzaa brewees of Mathare Valley', *African Urban Studies* (No. 3, Winter 1978–1979), 85–103.

OBI, S. N. C. *Modern Family Law in Southern Nigeria*. London, Sweet and Maxwell, 1966.

O'BRIEN, DENISE. 'Female husbands in Southern Bantu societies', in *Sexual Stratification*, Alice Schlegel (ed.), New York, Columbia University Press, 1977, pp. 109–26.

ODED, ARYE. *Islam in Uganda*, New York, John Wiley & Sons, 1974.

OKEDIJI, F. O., and O. O. OKEDIJI. 'Marital stability and social structure in an

African city', *The Nigerian Journal of Economic and Social Studies*, 8 (1966), 151–63.

OKEYO, ACHOLA PALA. 'Daughters of the lakes and rivers', in *Women and Colonization*, E. M. Etienne and Eleanor Leacock (eds), New York, Praeger, 1980, pp. 186–213.

OPPONG, CHRISTINE. *Marriage among a Matrilineal Elite*, Cambridge, Cambridge University Press, 1974; later published as *Middle Class African Marriage*, London, George Allen & Unwin, 1981.

OPPONG, C. (ed.) *Marriage, fertility and parenthood in West Africa*, Canberra, Australian National University, 1978.

ORUBULOYE, I. O. *Abstinence as a Method of Birth Control*, Canberra, Australian National University, 1981a.

ORUBULOYE, I. O. 'Education and socio-demographic change in Nigeria', in *Women, Education and Modernization of the Family in West Africa*, Helen Ware (ed.), Canberra, Australian National University, 1981b, pp. 22–41.

PARKIN, DAVID. 'Types of urban African marriage in Kampala', in *Africa and Change*, Colin Turnbull (ed.), New York, Alfred A. Knopf, 1973, pp. 208–26.

PEIL, MARGARET. 'Female roles in West African towns', in *Changing Social Structure in Ghana*, Jack Goody (ed.), London, International African Institute, 1975, pp. 73–90.

POEWE, KARLA. 'Matriliny in the throes of change: kinship, descent, and marriage in Luapula, Zambia', Part 1, *Africa* 48 (No. 4, 1978), 353–67.

POULTER, SEBASTIAN. 'The choice of law dilemma in Lesotho', in *Law and the Family in Africa*, Simon Roberts (ed.), The Hague, Paris, Mouton, 1977, pp. 169–82.

RANGER, TERENCE. 'Missionary adaptation of African religious institutions', in *The Historical Study of African Religions*, T. O. Ranger and Isaria Kimambo (eds), London, Heinemann, 1972, pp. 221–51.

ROBERTS, SIMON. *Botswana I: Tswana Family Law. Restatement of African Law*, London, Sweet & Maxwell, 1972.

ROBINS, CATHERINE. 'Conversion, life crises and stability among women in the East African Revival', in *The New Religions of Africa*, B. Jules-Rosette (ed.), Norwood, N.J., Ablex Publishing Co., 1979, pp. 185–202.

RYS, VLADIMIR. 'Problems of social security planning in developing countries', in *The African Social Security Series*. Fifth African Regional Conference of the International Social Security Association, held at Nairobi, 1974; International Social Security Association, General Secretariat, Geneva, 1975, pp. 25–37.

SCANZONI, JOHN. 'Social processes and power in families', in *Contemporary Theories about the Family*, Wesley Burr *et al* (eds), Vol. I, New York, Free Press, 1979, pp. 295–316.

SEMBAJWE, I. S. *Fertility and Infant Mortality amongst the Yoruba in Western Nigeria*, Canberra, Australian National University, 1981.

SENNETT, RICHARD. *Families against the City*, New York, Vintage Books, 1970.

SIBISI, HARRIET. 'How African women cope with migrant labour in South

Africa', in *Women and National Development*, Wellesley Editorial Committee (eds.) Chicago, University of Chicago Press, 1977, pp. 167–77.

SMOCK, AUDREY CHAPMAN. 'The impact of modernization on women's position in the family in Ghana', in *Sexual Stratification,* Alice Schlegel (ed.), New York, Columbia University Press, 1977, pp. 192–214.

SPREY, JETSE. 'Conflict theory and the study of marriage and the family', in *Theories about the Family*, Wesley Burr *et al.* (eds), Vol. II, New York, Free Press, 1979, pp. 130–59.

STROEBEL, MARGARET. *Muslim Women in Mombasa, 1890–1975*, New Haven, Conn., Yale University Press, 1979.

TESSEMA, H. E. and ATO GETAHN. 'Opening address', in *Development of Human Resources* by Ethiopian Council of Social Welfare, Nairobi, Afropress, 1971, pp. 9–15.

VAN ALLEN, JUDITH. '"Sitting on a Man": colonialism and the lost political institutions of Igbo women', *African Studies Review* 6 (1972), 165–81.

VAUGHAN, MEGAN. 'Which family? Problems in the reconstruction of the history of the family as an economic and cultural unit.' *Journal of African History*, 24 (2), 1983, pp. 275–84.

WARE, HELEN (ed.). *Women, Education and Modernization of the Family in West Africa,* Canberra, Australian National University, 1981.

WELCH, CHARLES E. and PAUL GLICK. 'The incidence of polygamy in contemporary Africa', *Journal of Marriage and the Family* 43 (Feb, 1981), 191–93.

WILSON, MONICA. *For Men and Elders*, London, International African Institute, 1977.

WINANS, E. V. 'The Shambala family', in *The Family Estate*, R. F. Gray and P. H. Gulliver (eds), London, Routledge & Kegan Paul, 1964, pp. 35–61.

WINCH, ROBERT, F. 'Toward a model of familial organization', in *Contemporary Theories about the Family*, Burr *et al.*, Vol. I, New York, Free Press, 1979, pp. 162–79.

ZELDITCH MORRIS. 'Role differentiation in the nuclear family', in *Family: Socialization and Interaction Process*, Talcott Parsons and Robert Bales, London, Routledge & Kegan Paul, 1956, pp. 307–52.

Suggestions for further reading

Chapter 1: Introduction: the family in Africa

CHRISTENSEN, H. T. (ed.) *Handbook of Marriage and the Family*, Chicago, Rand McNally & Co., 1964.

CLIGNET, REMI, and JOYCE SWEEN. 'Traditional and modern life styles in Africa', *Journal of Comparative Family Studies* 11 (Autumn 1971), 188–214.

DALTON, G. 'Bridewealth versus brideprice', *American Anthropologist* (June 1966).

HENIN, R. 'Marriage patterns in African nomadic groups', *Africa* 39 (No. 3, 1969), 238–59.

JACOBS, A. 'Masai marriage and bridewealth', *Mila* (1970), 25–36.

JOURNAL OF AFRICAN HISTORY, special issue *The history of the family in Africa*, 24(2) 1983, pp. 1455–288.

MAIR, LUCY. *African Marriage and Social Change*, London, Cass, 1969.

OKEDIJI, F. 'Some social psychological aspects of fertility among married women in an African city', *Nigerian Journal of Economic and Social Studies* 9 (No. 1, 1967), 67–79.

PAULME, DENISE (ed.). *Women of Tropical Africa*, Berkeley, Cal., University of California Press, 1963, pp. 47–92.

POOL, JANET. 'A cross-comparative study of conjugal behaviour in three West African countries', *Canadian Journal of African Studies* 6 (No. 2, 1972), 233–66.

UCHENDU, VICTOR. 'Concubinage among Ngwa Igbo of Southern Nigeria', *Africa* 35 (April 1965), 187–97.

WEEKES-VAGLIANI, WINIFRED. 'Some explanations of high fertility among rural women in Southern Cameroon', in *The Persistence of High Fertility*, John Caldwell (ed.), Canberra, Australian National University, 1977, pp. 451–65.

Chapter 2: Internal processes of the family

ALBERT, ETHEL. 'Women of Burundi', in *Women of Tropical Africa*, Denise Paulme (ed.), Berkeley, Cal., University of California Press, 1963, pp. 179–215.

BEIDELMAN, THOMAS. *The Matrilineal Peoples of Eastern Tanzania*, London, International African Institute, 1967.

BRAIN, JAMES. 'Less than second class: women in rural settlement schemes', in *Women in Africa*. Nancy J. Hafkin and Edna Bay, Stanford, Cal., Stanford University, 1976, pp. 265–82.

BRAIN, JAMES. 'Matrilineal descent and marital stability', *Journal of Asian and African Studies* 4 (No. 2, 1969), 122–31.

CAPLAN, PATRICIA and JANET BUJRA (eds). *Women United, Women Divided,* London, Tavistock Publications, 1978.

GRAYSHON, M. C. and OLANLOKEEN. 'Authority patterns in the Yoruba family', *West African Journal of Education* 10 (No. 3, 1966), 113–18.

HILTON, ANNE. 'Family and kinship among the Kongo south of the Zaire river from the sixteenth to the nineteenth centuries', *Journal of African History* 24(2), 1983 pp. 189–206.

LLOYD, P. C. 'Divorce among the Yoruba', *American Anthropologist* 70 (No. 1, 1968), 67–81.

PHIRI, KINGS, M. 'Some changes in the matrilineal family system of Malawi since the nineteenth century, *Journal of African History*, 24(2) 1983, pp. 257–74.

QUIMBY, LUCY. 'Islam, sex roles and modernization in Bobo-Dioulasso', in *The New Religions of Africa*, B. Jules-Rosette (ed.), Norwood, N.J., Ablex Publishing Co., 1979, pp. 203–18.

RAPAPORT, RHONA and ROBERT, and ZIONA STRELITZ. *Fathers, Mothers and Others*, London, Routledge & Kegan Paul, 1977.

URDANG, STEPHANIE. 'Fighting two colonialisms: the women's struggle in Guinea-Bissau', *African Studies Review* 18 (No. 3, 1975), 29–34.

WEISNER, THOMAS and RONALD GALLIMORE. 'My brother's keeper: child and sibling caretaking', *Current Anthropology* 18 (June 1977), 169–90.

Chapter 3: The family and society

ADEPOJU, ADERANTI. 'Migration and socio-economic links between urban migrants and home communities in Nigeria', *Africa* 44 (Oct. 1974), 383–95.

BARROWS, W. 'Rural–urban alliances and reciprocity in Africa', *Canadian Journal of African Studies* 5 (No. 3, 1971), 307–25.

BREESE, GERALD. *Urbanization in Newly Developing Countries*, Englewood Cliffs, N. J., Prentice-Hall, 1966.

BUKH, JETTE. *The Village Woman in Ghana*, Uppsala, Scandinavian Institute of African Studies, 1979.

CHILDS, S. 'Christian marriage in Nigeria', *Africa* 16 (No. 4, 1946).

DENYER, SUSAN. *African Traditional Architecture*, London, Heinemann, 1978.

DOBKIN, M. 'Colonialism and the legal status of women in Francophonic Africa', *Cahiers d'Etudes Africaines* 8 (1968), 390–405.

FRAENKEL, MERRAN. *Tribe and Class in Monrovia*, London, International African Institute, 1964.

GOODY, J. 'Class and marriage in Africa and Eurasia', *American Journal of Sociology* 76 (No. 4, 1971), 585–603.

GUGLER, J. 'The second sex in town', *Canadian Journal of African Studies* 6 (No. 2, 1972), 284–302.

GUTTO, S. B. O. 'The status of women in Kenya', Discussion Paper No. 235, Institute for Development Studies, University of Nairobi, Nairobi, April 1976.

GUTTO, S. B. O. (ed.). 'Children and the law in Kenya', Occasional Paper No. 35, Institute for Development Studies, University of Nairobi, Nairobi, July 1979.

GUYER, JANE I. 'Food, cocoa, and the division of labour by sex in two West African societies', *Comparative Studies in Society and History* 22 (July 1980), 355–73.

HANDWERKER, W. 'Kinship, friendship and business failure among market sellers in Monrovia', *Africa* 43 (1973), 288–301.

KALANDA, PAUL. 'Adaptations of church law to the Ganda marriage prohibitions', *African Ecclesiastical Review* 5 (No. 1, 1963, 39–49.

KRIGE, EILEEN J. 'Traditional and Christian Lovedu family structures', in *Religion and Social Change in Southern Africa*, Michael Whisson and Martin West (eds), London, Rex Collings, 1975, 129–52.

MITCHELL, CLYDE. 'Social networks', *Annual Review of Anthropology* 3 (1974), 279–399.

NAFZIGER, E. W. 'The effect of the Nigerian extended family on entrepreneurial activity', *Economic Development and Cultural Change* 18 (1969), 25–33.

OUSMANE, SEMBENE. *God's Bits of Wood,* London, Heinemann, 1962.

ROBERTS, SIMON (ed.). *Law and the Family in Africa*, The Hague, Paris, Mouton, 1977.

ROUSSEAU, IDA FAYE. 'African women's identity crisis? some observations on education and the changing role of women in Sierra Leone and Zaire', in *Women Cross-Culturally: Change and Challenge*, Ruby Rohrlich-Leavitt (ed.), The Hague, Paris, Mouton, 1975, pp. 41–52.

VAN ALLEN, JUDITH. 'Memsahib, militante, femme libre: political and apolitical styles of modern African women', in *Women in Politics,* J. S. Jacquette (ed.), New York, John Wiley & Sons. 1974, pp. 304–21.

WARE, HELEN. 'Security in the city: the role of the family in urban West Africa', in *The Economic and Social Supports for High Fertility*, Lado Ruzicka (ed.), Canberra, Australian National University, 1977, pp. 385–408.

WHITING, BEATRICE. 'Changing life styles in Kenya', *Daedalus* 106 (No. 2, 1977), 211–26.

Chapter 4: Conflict and the family

CALDWELL, J. C. *African Rural–Urban Migration, the Movement to Ghana's Towns*, Canberra, Australian National University Press, 1969.

CARLEBACH, J. 'Family relationships of deprived and non-deprived Kikuyu children from polygamous marriages', *Journal of Tropical Paediatrics* 13 (No. 4, 1967), 185–200.

CLIFFORD, W. *A Primer of Social Case Work in Africa*, Lusaka, Oxford University Press, 1966.

COHEN, RONALD. 'Marital instability among the Kanuri of Northern Nigeria', *American Anthropologist* 63 (1961), 6.

DAVISON, E. H. *Social Case Work*, London, Billing and Sons, 1966.

EGERTON, R. 'The shaming party among the Pokot of East Africa', *South-western Journal of Anthropology* 20 (No. 4, 1964), 404–18.

FALLERS, LLOYD. 'Determinants of marital stability in Busoga.' *Africa* 27 (No. 2, 1957), 106–24.

MINUCHIN, SALVADOR. *Families and Family Therapy*, London, Tavistock Publications, 1974.

OKEYO, ACHOLA PALA, 'Women in the household economy: Management of multiple roles', *Studies in Family Planning* 10 (No. 11/12, Nov./Dec. 1979).

OLUSANYA, P. 'Factors affecting stability of marriage among Yoruba', *Journal of Marriage and the Family* 32 (No. 1, 1970), 150–61.

OPPONG, C. 'A note from Ghana on chains of change in family systems and Family Size', *Journal of Marriage and the Family* (Aug. 1977), 615–21.

POTASH, BETTY. 'Some aspects of marital stability in a rural Luo community', *Africa* 48 (No. 4, 1978), 380–97.

SANGREE WALTER, 'Going home to mother', *American Anthropologist* 71 (No. 6, 1969), 1046–57.

SATIR, VIRGINIA. *Conjoint Family Therapy*, London, Souvenir Press, 1978.

SKINNER, E. 'Inter-generational conflict among the Masai', *Journal of Conflict Resolution* 5 (1961), 55–60.

SPECHT, H. and VICKERY, A. *Integrating Social Work Methods*, London, George Allen Unwin, 1977.

Chapter 5: Areas of family policy in Africa

ELLIS, J. 'Different conceptions of a child's needs: some implications for social work with West African children and their parents', *British Journal of Social Work* 7 (no. 2. 1977). 155—71.

HILL, REUBEN, *et al.* (eds) *The Family and Population Control: a Puerto Rican Experiment in Social Change*, Chapel Hill, N.C., University of North Carolina Press, 1959, ch. 13 on 'Implications of the research for commonwealth policies and programmes', pp. 365–89, and ch. 7 on 'Selected family types and fertility control', pp. 191–217.

INTERNATIONAL ASSOCIATION OF SCHOOLS OF SOCIAL WORK, *Education for Family Welfare: a Component of Development* IASSW, New York, 1977.

KAMERMAN, SHEILA and ALFRED KOHN (eds). *Family Policy*. New York, Columbia University Press, 1978.

KULKARNI, P. D., 'The Development Function and Interdisciplinary Nature of Social Welfare', in *Education for Social Change: Human Development and National Progress* by IASSW, New York, 1975, pp. 24–33.

NYE, F. IVAN, and GERALD W. McDONALD. 'Family policy: emergent models and some theoretical issues', *Journal of Marriage and the Family* 41 (Aug. 1979), 473–86.

PERSHING, B. 'Family policies: a component of management in the home and family setting', *Journal of Marriage and the Family* 41 (Aug. 1979), 573–81.

ZAMBIA COUNCIL ON SOCIAL WELFARE, *The Role of Social Welfare Services in Rural Development.* Nairobi, Prudential Printers, 1973.

Chapter 6: Theoretical considerations

HANDWERKER, W. PENN. 'Family, fertility and economics', *Current Anthropology* 18 (June 1977), 259–87.

LANE, ANN. 'Women in society: a critique of Frederick Engels', in *Liberating Women's History: Theoretical and Critical Essays*, B. A. Carroll, London, University of Illinois Press, 1976, pp. 4–25.

MORGAN, D. H. J. *Social Theory and the Family*, London, Routledge & Kegan Paul, 1975.

NYE, F. I. *Role Structure and Analysis of the Family*, London, Sage Publications, 1976.

Index